# Wising Up
## Applying the Wisdom of Proverbs
## to Daily Life

Sisters: Bible Study for Women

*Knowing God:*
*Making God the Main Thing in My Life*
by Kimberly Dunnam Reisman

*Unfailing Love:*
*Growing Closer to Jesus Christ*
by Rebecca Laird

*Finding Balance:*
*Loving God with Heart and Soul, Mind and Strength*
by Becca Stevens

*A Mile in Her Shoes:*
*Lessons from the Lives of Old Testament Women*
by Sheron C. Patterson

*Wising Up:*
*Applying the Wisdom of Proverbs to Daily Life*
by Cheryl A. Kirk-Duggan

Sisters
Bible Study for Women

# Wising Up

## Applying the Wisdom of Proverbs to Daily Life

**Participant's Workbook**

Cheryl A. Kirk-Duggan

**Abingdon Press / Nashville**

SISTERS
WISING UP: APPLYING THE WISDOM OF PROVERBS TO DAILY LIFE

*Copyright © 2005 by Cheryl A. Kirk-Duggan*

All rights reserved.
No part of this work may be reproduced or transmitted in any form or by any means, electronic or mechanical, including photocopying and recording, or by any information storage or retrieval system, except as may be expressly permitted by the 1976 Copyright Act or in writing from the publisher. Requests for permission should be addressed in writing to Abingdon Press, 201 Eighth Avenue South, Nashville, TN 37203, or e-mail: *permissions@abingdonpress.com.*

*This book is printed on acid-free, elemental chlorine-free paper.*

**Library of Congress Cataloging-in-Publication Data**

Kirk-Duggan, Cheryl A.
    Wising up : applying the wisdom of Proverbs to daily life : participant's workbook / Cheryl A. Kirk-Duggan.
    p. cm.
    Includes bibliographical references.
    ISBN 0-687-05396-X (binding: adhesive : alk. paper)
    1. Bible. O.T. Proverbs—Meditations. 2. Devotional calendars. 3. African American women—Prayer-books and devotions—English. I. Title.

    BS1465.54.K57 2005
    223'.7'0071—dc22

                        2005007477

Scripture quotations from New Revised Standard Version of the Bible, copyright 1989, Division of Christian Education of the National Council of Churches of Christ in the United States of America. Used by permission. All rights reserved.

ISBN 978-0-687-05396-4

My deepest thanks and blessings
to some who have nurtured and inspired me on the way:

Rebecca Brooks, my departed maternal grandmother
Naomi Ruth Moseley Kirk, my departed mother
Rudolph V. Kirk, my departed father
Edna Daniels, my maternal aunt
Dedurie V. Kirk, my beloved sister
Jessie Katherine Wilson, my sister-mother friend
Michelle Hall Williams, my special daughter
Faye M. Morris, sister-friend
Diane Thomas, sister-friend
Marsha Foster Boyd, sister-friend
Louise Noel, sister-friend
Mike Kirk-Duggan, beloved husband and occasional editor

# Contents

# Introduction

*Who has ascended to heaven and come down?*
*Who has gathered the wind in the hollow of the hand?*
*Who has wrapped up the waters in a garment?*
*Who has established all the ends of the earth?*
*What is the person's name?*
*And what is the name of the person's child?*
*Surely you know!*

*(Proverbs 30:4)*

Knowing is a process of becoming familiar with new ideas, concepts, and experiences. That process and what we discern are beautiful gifts from God. One of the biblical categories of knowledge that affects our daily lives is the material known as *Wisdom Literature*. Wisdom Literature is a modern critical term about writing in ancient Israel and throughout the ancient Near East. Wisdom Literature concerns pedagogy or teaching, because the intent behind these materials is to convey basic truth about life and therefore offer a way of understanding the world. Intimate to Wisdom Literature is an underlying belief that despite all the apparent confusion, injustice, and disorder of life and the world, there is a basic pattern, an ordering by which all such phenomena can ultimately be understood. Because of confusions, uncertainties, and mysteries concerning life that arise, one of the core virtues of wisdom is patience. One desires to take the path or way of the sage and not the fool. Being wise, however, does not protect one from experiencing suffering. The biblical books grouped under the heading of Wisdom Literature include the Song of Songs, Ecclesiastes, Job, and Proverbs.

The Song of Songs, also known as the Song of Solomon or the Canticle of Canticles, is a book that contains brief, sensual, musical, erotic love poems in which two people express their intensely subjective experience using sexually provocative language and imagery of love, passion, desire, and longing. Significantly, the woman, not a narrator, shares her story in her own voice through monologues, soliloquies, and love songs. Here, *wisdom* embraces the sensual, sexual side of life, echoing Genesis 1, where God created humanity and said that we are good. In the Song of Songs, we learn that the body is good, as is being mutually responsible, sensual, and sexually intimate with one's mature, committed lover.

The Book of Ecclesiastes is a nontraditional Wisdom book, apparently collected by a cynic, in which the Qoheleth (the preacher), speaks in favor of the human condition. In this book, true wisdom is elusive and may ultimately be unavailable. Through this book, wisdom teaches that is it better to know that answers may *not* be forthcoming, rather than to fall into the trap of easy answers. We might be wiser to accept life without trying to analyze its meaning, to live the best we can and leave judgment to God, whose ways are not always clear.

Job is a drama that begins with God and Satan making a wager about a righteous man named Job. The book continues with a series of dialogues between Job and his friends or comforters. They use their own particular wisdom traditions as they try to comfort Job and help him accept his suffering as part of God's just plan, regardless of the depths of Job's pain and loss. Because of the wager, Job endures great personal tragedy and physical agony. While Job's friends espouse wisdom, Job challenges it. Job has lived all of his life as a righteous man and is troubled by the suffering he experiences. In the end, he is wise, for he yields to God, allowing God to have the last word. We too can become wise here in learning that there is order despite suffering and that, in the words of Rabbi Kushner, bad things do happen to good people.

## Proverbs

The Book of Proverbs, the subject of this study, contains short, pithy sayings contained within collections of axioms or principles that offer counsel and guidance. Some proverbs are regional, while others span the globe; some are part of oral traditions; and some are contained in sacred texts like the Bible and the

Qur'an. Proverbs reflect people's traditional ways of experiencing life and reality. Proverbs reflect the assumed or proper way of doing things. Proverbs are about the values, admonitions, rules, and insights that parents and elders desire their young to embrace. The construction of proverbs—short and sassy with a punch line as a conclusion—makes them easy to memorize. People from all walks of life and various cultures throughout time, from celebrated thinkers and philosophers to everyday villagers, have created proverbs. Proverbs of all sorts teach the wisdom of morality, espousing virtues from honesty to patience to righteousness.

Although in this book we will use the biblical Book of Proverbs, such succinct statements are present in many other sacred writings. Consider a *Hadith* from Sufism. A *Hadith* might be a report of what the prophet said, did, approved or disapproved of. The collection of the deeds, practices, and words of the prophet—known from the Hadiths—is called the *Sunnah,* and forms the second source of Islamic law after the Qur'an. Following are a few Hadiths:

- Divine breezes from your Lord waft through the days of your life. Listen! Be aware of them.
- Have mercy on people so you may receive mercy; forgive people so you may be forgiven.
- The first stage of worship is silence.
- Avoid greed, for greed in itself is poverty.
- The strongest among you is the one who controls his anger.
- Protect and honor the earth, for the earth is like your mother.
- Avoid stubbornness, for it begins in ignorance and ends in regret.
- The cure of ignorance is to ask and learn.
- Trust in God, but tie your camel's leg.
- Heaven lies under the feet of mothers.
- God exalts the humble and humbles the proud.

(*Essential Sufism,* by James Fadiman and Robert Frager; Harper Collins)

Proverbs, taken from the Wisdom Books of the Hebrew Bible (Old Testament) represent centuries of instruction from ancient Israel and were developed in the home, schools, and royal courts of David and Solomon. These Proverbs do not focus on major religious themes such as Exodus, patriarchal families, or covenant, as found in other parts of the Hebrew Bible. Instead the Book of Proverbs contains short sayings, comparisons, and similitudes that express the practical wisdom and experience of the ancient Israelites. Interestingly, the word *wisdom* appears forty-two times in the Book of Proverbs.

The Book of Proverbs proclaims that there is order in the world; that God is in charge, and thus a relationship with God is where one begins to attain wisdom. This order exists even when the world and our own personal and communal realities seem chaotic, for wisdom is integral to God's birthing of creation. Proverbs supply people with concrete, everyday values and information so that they can make better decisions. Proverbs help us live in a meaningful way and teach us about a disciplined life. These sayings alert us to the fact that there are consequences to our actions. According to the Proverbs, there are two ways in life: blessed or cursed. Thus, the Book of Proverbs contrasts the way of God's righteous children with the life of the wicked. The blessings and curses that appear throughout Proverbs occur individually and communally. The brevity of the sayings allows for easy recall as one moves about daily life. Unfortunately, the archaic language of the proverbs, as well as their meaning, is often difficult for modern people to comprehend and apply.

The Book of Proverbs was not written by one person in a systematic way. These proverbs arise from several ancient traditions in which the sages wanted to coin short sayings that could help guide their community and the generations to come. Many people assume that the sages who wrote these sayings were men; in fact, over the years people have used the Proverbs, especially Proverbs 31 (a poem on how to find a capable wife), to justify controlling, limiting, and categorizing women. In Hebrew, Spirit is *ruach* and Wisdom is *chomak*. How ironic, then, that Sophia, Wisdom, the name for the Holy Spirit in Hebrew, in which nouns are gender specific, is a feminine name for God, and the Hebrew writings that contain proverbs are collectively known as Wisdom Literature.

In this book we will use the theology and ethics of many of the biblical proverbs to provide insight and resources for women, helping them to live a transformed life in which each woman can place herself in relationship with God, joyously relinquishing the language of sacrifice and male gratification. As you complete this study, my hope is that you will have gained tools to support your experience of self-empowerment in a walk that is close to God and to possess a heightened love for and awareness of the female self in daily living.

## ABOUT THE STUDY

*Wising Up* is a six-week Bible study designed for group use. For each of the six weeks, this book provides daily readings and activities for group participants. On the last day of each week, there will be a group meeting, where participants will watch and discuss a video.

The daily study segments in this book have four parts: (1) the biblical text, (2) comments on the text, (3) questions for reflecting and recording, and (4) a "daughter-friend moment." For this last part, we suggest that you find a younger woman (teenage or older) with whom you can have a conversation and engage in spiritual exercises.

Please set aside thirty minutes to an hour each day for Bible study. I suggest after reading the text for the day that you spend a few minutes meditating on it. Next, read the overview, which contains reflections on the text, its themes, and application to daily living. Then move to the four questions that accompany each study, and answer them out of your experiences and unique relationship with God. The questions and daughter-friend moments include at least one of the following opportunities built into each day, based upon the reading for that day:

- An applied challenge (for example, select one verse or concept and live its principles today);
- A creative moment (write a poem, prayer, short story, proverb, or song);
- A teaching moment (share your thoughts and insights);
- A reflecting moment (list what you enjoyed, understood, or found puzzling);
- A moment of biblical interpretation involving opportunities for creative being and doing (for example, select three verses and rewrite them in your own words).

Writing this Bible study on Proverbs has been a marvelous journey of discovery and joy; and I hope that as you engage in this six-week study, you too will have a journey of discovery, empowerment, and transformation. As you work daily with this Bible study, I pray that your walk with God will be more intimate and that you will experience renewal. As you read, study, and reflect, please take note of the various Wisdom sayings and observe the daily use of wisdom in your own life.

At the completion of the study, my hope is that you will be more mindful of the use of wisdom each day and of the wisdom sayings that you have grown up with. For example, one of the sayings that my Grannie frequently used was, "Pot can't call kettle black, and okra can't call pepper long mouth." In other words, before we criticize someone else, we need to be aware of our own behaviors. In reflecting on women's wisdom, we have the opportunity to connect familial wisdom with that of the Bible.

I trust that as you complete this study, you will come to love yourself in deeper ways. In placing your relationship with God first, my hope is that you will not only come to love yourself, God, and your neighbor but that you will also develop relationships that are deeply supportive of your own well-being. Most important, I hope that during this journey you will have an opportunity to reflect on every aspect of your life in a way that will help you achieve a more balanced, healthy life. Blessings as you embrace *Wising Up!*

# Week One: Daily Applied Understanding

## DAY ONE: KNOWLEDGE

*Let the wise also hear and gain in learning, / and the discerning acquire skill / to understand a proverb and a figure, / the words of the wise and their riddles. / The [awe] of the LORD is the beginning of knowledge; / fools despise wisdom and instruction. / Hear, my child, your father's instruction, / and do not reject your mother's teaching.*

*(Proverbs 1:5-8)*

Some mornings I awaken and am astounded by the awesomeness of God. When I go for an early morning walk, I marvel at the artistry and architecture of God. Certainly the sages of old experienced the same kind of feeling and wonderment about God. Such an experience serves as a warning, a caveat for getting us in touch with the experience of wisdom in a way that helps us carry a similar curiosity and awe about nature. Such an experience of nature can be with us throughout our daily experience, that we might know the gift, pleasure, and challenge of learning as holy practice. Knowing and learning, by God's grace, can help elevate us to new heights of experiencing and being with God, with ourselves, and with community.

Sometimes we approach new knowledge with trepidation and angst. We allow the unknown to agitate us, bringing up all kinds of self-doubt and feelings of low self-esteem. Wise women say that the more we learn, the more we know there is to learn. Although it is impossible for us to learn everything about everything, we need not let the reality of incomplete knowledge become an opportunity to beat ourselves up. We can be grateful for what we do know and never let a day pass that we don't actively seek to learn something new. For even if it were possible to have all knowledge, to learn everything about our universe and galaxy, learning for the sake of learning would be empty.

Proverbs teaches us that the epitome of learning is not about the acquisition of facts, or the accolades that such acquisition might bring, such as fame or fortune. The root of knowledge is about an encounter with God, about the "fear," awe, or respect of God. If respect for God is the beginning of knowledge and the capacity to learn is God-given, then the exercise of learning itself is *holy* business: What a revolutionary thought! Learning becomes liturgy and prayer, which affords us a deeper appreciation for the little things and the capacity to experience each moment as blessing.

Knowing that comes with blessing is an experience of love. Mechtild of Magdeburg, a 13th-century German mystic, author, and religious reformer, tells us in *The Flowing Light of the Godhead* that having tremendous knowledge without love means we can never fully embrace and know God or a godly life. Knowledge in and of itself will be like sounding brass and tinkling cymbals (1 Corinthians 13:1) but will not produce a rich tapestry or mosaic of moving sound. The *knowing* that embodies love and blessing is the context for commitment to a moral life. Living a moral life with joy and love is one of the gifts of wisdom. As we perceive and discern in new ways because of our conscious contact with God, we respect and love God more.

The gift of loving and respecting God signals the possibility for us to know, love, and respect ourselves. We begin to *hear* and *see* and *touch* and *taste* and *smell* in new ways. Our knowledge expands beyond written texts to the texts of art and culture, nature and science, and intimacy with ourselves. We learn to appreciate ourselves in ways we have never known. We can look into the eyes of the young and know a new sense of joy. We can peer into the eyes of our elders and know the grace of contentment. We begin to see the wisdom that our parents taught us. For the first time, we are also able to see our parents' shortcomings as well as their strengths and no longer hold their perceived weaknesses against them.

As we get to know God better, we can come to recognize the *Imago Dei,* the God presence within ourselves, and appreciate in a profound way that God has already pronounced that our being, our existence, is a *created* good. Then, each day becomes a new beginning. We can do things this day that we could never imagine doing for a lifetime. We can come to a new place of wisdom and experience of ourselves as a gift, in wonderment, love, and thanksgiving. We can be brave and step out on faith, leaning on the everlasting love and grace of God.

In sum, knowledge is a process of coming to understand more about God, our relationship with God, and about ourselves. In wisdom, we know that the more we learn the more there is to learn. We learn about texts, art, culture, nature, science, joy, and contentment. With enhanced encounter, learning and knowing become holy practice as we embrace God and life with love and respect.

## Reflecting and Recording

Who in your life would you consider a wise woman? Why? What attributes does she have that you want to emulate?

How would you define *wisdom* for a person of faith? Would you use the same definition if speaking to someone at work? If not, how would you alter your definition?

Do you exercise wisdom, particularly when it comes to loving yourself, in the persons whom you choose to be your friends? If not, think about and then list one criteria you might use for selecting friends from a wisdom perspective.

## Daughter-Friend Moment

Growing up in the 21st century is a challenging journey, but it can be rewarding rather than fraught with fear if we have friends and loved ones to walk with us. Think about your teenage or young adult daughter or another young woman—niece or goddaughter—whom you have befriended and care about. How would you explain to her the difference between loving and being intimate with a God you respect rather than a God who records mistakes in some eternal book?

# DAY TWO: RESPECT

*Because they hated knowledge / and did not choose the [awe] of the LORD, / would have none of my counsel, / and despised all my reproof, / therefore they shall eat the fruit of their way / and be sated with their own devices. / For waywardness kills the simple, / and the complacency of fools destroys them.*

*(Proverbs 1:29-32)*

We live in a world where knowledge is no longer a privilege but a necessity. Everything from books to groceries to furniture to doctor appointments is computerized. Our technically complex world requires reasonable competence with computers, word processors, electronic date books, and DVD and CD players. But knowledge about things is not a requirement for knowing God or having peace of mind. At the same time, when we exercise our faith, do we have to give up the wonderful world of knowledge? The sage of Proverbs 1:29-32 would say no!

Each moment each day, we have opportunities to make healthy decisions in freedom. God gives us the gift of freedom; and in getting that freedom, we need to practice wisdom and discernment. To reject knowledge is to choose to shut down, to live in a vacuum, to say we already know enough. We may not utter these words, but our attitudes and body language speak them for us. We may have a lot of information about a lot of things, but we don't know everything about anything. Without a doubt, we can never have total knowledge of God. God is mystery. As such, we can know God only as God chooses to self-reveal. What would we learn about God and ourselves if we chose to reveal our true selves to God and to someone we trust?

An inventory of our selves leads to true self-knowledge, which is the beginning of healing. When we reject knowledge about ourselves, ultimately we reject God. To say no to knowledge is to dismiss one of the inheritances that God gives us, the capacity to learn. To say no to knowledge and learning is to dismiss the joy and challenges of mentoring. To say no to knowledge is to rob another of the opportunity to help us.

Such an impoverished mindset can lead to an impoverished spirit, granting us permission never to grow up, never to face our chronic issues. Sometimes we so closely identify with our particular challenges that we become our own worst problem. Once this happens, the possibility for transformation diminishes greatly. We become exhausted and hopelessly tired and listless. We experience sorrow, grief, and fatigue because we have shut down our creativity and our lifeline to others and to God. We have refused to live in the moment.

Timing is crucial in the Wisdom tradition; for if we live in the moment, we can know God. We experience seasons in our lives, like the seasons of the year. In some geographic zones, the weather is always temperate, while in other areas, the weather tends to be cold. We, too, may feel as if we've been in one season forever. Often those of us in our spring years yearn for autumn; some of us resting in winter long for the summer of youth. When we live in the moment, we have little time to yearn for any moment other than the one that lies before us, appreciating what has happened in the past, celebrating the transformations of the present, and knowing that change will come in the future.

In the present moment of *now*—not then, not later, but now—the capacity to breathe, to sleep, to learn, and to show others involves a respect for knowledge and for self. We experience and celebrate the simple elegance of life with moment-to-moment awareness. We learn the lesson that today is the tomorrow that we feared yesterday. In practicing such respect for the gift of living, we become more aware of God and God's people, creativity, and new possibilities. Although we experience insensitivity, pain, suffering, and death, we can still cherish each moment. For we have an opportunity to learn, with praise and thanksgiving, looking to the hills for strength and assurance.

In sum, respect involves an awareness of homage to God and love of our selves. When we respect and love God, we are in covenant relationship; and we understand that God provides. When we respect and love ourselves, we can make healthy choices in freedom, can engage in learning, and can live, not fretting about the past and not being obsessed about the future. Respect is the context for negotiating life in a healthy manner.

## Reflecting and Recording

On a sheet of paper, make two columns. Write the word "Respect" at the top of one column and "Knowledge" at the top of the other. List words that come to mind about each word in the appropriate column. Meditate for a few moments afterwards; then review your list. Why did you write these particular words? What are the similarities and dissimilarities between the two lists?

Who are some people among your family and friends whose capacity for knowledge you admire? Why?

What one thing are you willing to do today that will improve your capacity for being open to knowledge about God?

## Daughter-Friend Moment

Think about your own personality when it comes to respecting yourself, God, and others. Do you have a set way of being with people, or do you adapt within the moment? How could you use the day's proverb to teach your daughter or a younger friend or colleague about the importance of knowledge and the keys to self-respect?

# DAY THREE: LISTENING

*My child, if you accept my words / and treasure up my commandments within you, /*
*making your ear attentive to wisdom / and inclining your heart to understanding;*
*/ if you indeed cry out for insight, / and raise your voice for understanding; . . .*
*then you will understand the [awe] of the* LORD */ and find the knowledge of God.*
*. . . For wisdom will come into your heart / and knowledge will be pleasant*
*to your soul; / prudence will watch over you; / and understanding will guard you. /*
*It will save you from the way of evil, / from those who speak perversely, . . . /*
*who rejoice in doing evil / and delight in the perverseness of evil; . . . /*
*You will be saved from the loose woman, / from the adulteress with her smooth words,*
*/ who forsakes the partner of her youth / and forgets her sacred covenant.*

*(Proverbs 2:1-3, 5, 10-12, 14, 16-17)*

Many observe that praying is talking to God, whereas meditation is listening to God speaking within us. Some would suggest that prayer is a dialogue; we make utterances, then we become quiet, that we might hear God's response.

What is the difference between *hearing* and *listening?* Sometimes we use the words synonymously, but they do not mean the same thing. To *hear* is the capacity to perceive sound through one's auditory sense; this is a physical phenomenon. People who cannot hear are deaf. To *listen* means that we pay attention to something. Paying attention to something we hear is the experience of listening. People who cannot listen are self-centered. Listening encompasses both the physical process and the attention we give to hearing that allows us to listen in a mental, emotional, and spiritual manner. And it is certainly true that many people who can hear do not listen.

22

When we listen to God and to others, we have an opportunity to treasure and live life being faithful to God's commandments, which can be summed up by loving God first, then ourselves, and then all others as we work to do justice, love mercy, and walk humbly with God (Micah 6:8). When we listen in this manner, we can do so creatively, intentionally, and lovingly. We can pay attention to the wisdom of those around us, the wisdom that has been written down, and the wisdom transmitted to us through tradition. With listening comes a greater capacity for understanding.

We listen well when we listen to our innermost selves. Wisdom comes from the heart, where the heart is a metaphor for a place where body, mind, and soul intersect. When these work in harmony, we are our healthiest selves. We are open to creative expression and to God's wisdom. And wisdom, in turn, helps us to avoid destructive behavior and negative people.

Who is the "loose woman" in today's proverb? The question becomes especially hard to answer when we realize that four women in the lineage of Mary, the mother of Jesus, might have been categorized that way: Tamar, Rahab, Ruth, and the wife of Uriah (Bathsheba). Although the text appears primarily to pertain to fidelity in marriage, it might be that in reality it refers to humanity's response to Wisdom, who is female. Put another way, are we faithful to Sophia, to Wisdom?

Osage women say that in making a footprint, they live in the light of day. To live in the light of day is to have a heightened sensory awareness of one's reality: to smell deeply, to touch with compassion, to hear in splendor, to see beyond measure, to taste the ambrosia of the gods. A traditional song, based on 1 John 1:5, says it in another way:

> *We'll walk in the light, [the] beautiful light.*
> *[We'll] come where the dewdrops of mercy are bright.*
> *[Jesus will] shine all around us by day and by night:*
> *Jesus, the Light of the world.*

To have wisdom one must listen well, for what is said and what remains unspoken.

Listening will help us remember and embrace our sacred covenant with God and with each other. Have we listened well and discerned where we are to take our rightful place? Do we spend time in meditation so that we might listen uninterrupted to God, to the Wisdom of the Ages? Because each day is new and is full of moments when we can listen to God, we need not worry or fret. God's wisdom is available for us. We can embrace this wisdom and listen to how our communities need us to minister to them, and they to us.

Do we think enough of ourselves to take on listening more faithfully as we break out of our malaise and listen to the God within us, the God who is around us, the God who will grant us the ability to know peace?

Thus, to listen is to pay attention to the divine and the human as we live in community and in relationship. To listen is to be faithful to wisdom, committing to live in harmony, synchronicity, and love as an act and work of justice and mercy, and to be humble before God. Listening affords us the opportunity to experience revelation, to better know God, and ultimately, as we listen to the God inside, to hear and love ourselves.

## Reflecting and Recording

Observe and take note of how others are interacting with you. Notice how often people hear you and how often they really listen. Observing a person's eyes will tell you a great deal.

Choose two different selections from favorite CDs. As you listen to the songs, observe yourself and note the musical elements that you find appealing as well as those you find unappealing.

Find a public place where you can observe and listen to others for fifteen or twenty minutes. When you listen in a public setting, what do you learn about human nature? What do you learn about yourself and your capacity to listen?

**Daughter-Friend Moment**

How would you explain the difference between listening and hearing to your daughter-friend in a way that can be illuminating and helpful as she builds relationships with others? How can you help her learn to discern between listening to others, to herself, and to the God within, integrating the best wisdom of the three? Together test your ability to communicate by translating Proverbs 2:1-3, 5 into your own words.

# DAY FOUR: TRUST

*Trust in the LORD with all your heart, / and do not rely on your own insight. / In all your ways acknowledge [the LORD], / and [the LORD] will make straight your paths. / Do not be wise in your own eyes; / [have awe of] the LORD, and turn away from evil. / It will be a healing for your flesh / and a refreshment for your body.*

*(Proverbs 3:5-8)*

Trust is one of those words that is weighted and tied up with faith, well-being, and relationships. Some of us misplace our trust and become wounded and feel betrayed. Sometimes we can identify feelings of misplaced trust and are aware of betrayals by significant others. Others sometimes tell us that we have not been wronged, that we only feel that way, thus sending the message that our feelings are irrelevant or inconsequential. After having an experience of being wronged, abused, misused, and disrespected, it becomes more difficult to trust anyone, even God. We begin to ask, if God is real and loving and powerful, why would God allow bad, hurtful things to happen to us?

Some of us have not yet arrived at asking this question of God, because we have not yet named our pain and the betrayal. If we have experienced being wronged and betrayed many times, we may be in denial as a means of survival. Such experiences make us numb so that we are no longer conscious of pain. Sometimes the only way to survive an untenable situation is to repress it and pretend it never happened, or that it is inconsequential and does not matter, so that we can get on with more important bits and pieces of our lives. In wrestling with trust, we have the opportunity to unearth some of this pain and come to a point of awareness. With awareness comes the opportunity to connect with people who can help us get well. Part of getting well is to begin to experience trust with others once again.

Trust is always about relationships: relationships between God and us, between individuals, between particular individuals and a particular community, and between different communities, all for particular purposes. Trust denotes dependence. We trust God, for we know ultimately that no one can always be there for us other than God. Even with the best intentions, our loved ones cannot always be fully present for us. In some instances, they ought *not* to be always or fully present for us. Codependency means "being there" for another or others, without requiring those persons to "be there" for us, in a mutual relationship. To trust in another means to have a feeling of certainty that we can depend upon someone or something. To trust means we have assurance and confidence that a person or a thing is sure, there, and unfailing. Such a trust theologically is the power of covenant. God made a covenant with Abram (Genesis 12:1-3), to have a relationship with Abram's kinfolk in perpetuity, to give him land, and to give him a son. As believers, we also have a covenant with God through the revelation of Jesus the Christ. Jesus' new covenant is an understanding with believers wherein Jesus promises that the Holy Spirit will give us all the wisdom, encouragement, capacity for transformation, and love for God and our neighbor that we need. In and of ourselves we do not have the capacity for such wisdom, knowledge, or power to change. Moreover, there are also legal trusts, where one person (trustee) holds something, for example, property, for the benefit of another (beneficiary). We hold relationships such as the pastor/parishioner, attorney/client, and doctor/patient as trusts. We have an expectation, faith, and/or a belief that what has been said within those relationships will be held in strictest confidence.

While these relationships are important, the poet of the Proverbs tells us to locate our trust in God. We can trust God to help us discern and enter into relationship with others who are worthy of our trust. With our own naked eye, our insight can be skewed and misplaced. The lens we peer through may be distorted, scratched, or warped. In connecting with God, we come to realize that the voice within warns us when we cannot trust another. With time, we learn to trust the Spirit within to let us know whom we can or cannot trust. When we trust God, we can experience every moment of life as a holy, sacred time, regardless of the task at hand.

Trusting God's wisdom means we can take the time to be holy and speak with God often, as many times as we need to during a 24-hour period. To trust God's wisdom means to be self-aware, not self-centered. To be self-centered is to be so consumed with the self that we disconnect from God. When we disconnect from God, we cannot love ourselves. Loving God goes hand-in-hand with loving ourselves. Loving ourselves allows us to love our neighbor. Through trust in God, we can then tap into the collective wisdom of the ages. To be wise means to be wise through grace. Trusting God is part of the matrix of loving and respecting God. Respecting or fearing God (not in the sense of being afraid of but as a way of holding God in highest esteem) provides us with the wherewithal to turn away from evil and negativity.

The beauty of trusting God (leaning and depending on God so that God is the most important reality in our lives) is that it is the beginning of our capacity to heal. The love of God is so incredibly powerful, pure, and present that we know that through grace we are worthy to be loved and that we are lovable. With this realization come renewal, refreshment, and rejuvenation. With this shift and transformation, we are able to confess the wrongs we have done and the wrongs done to us; we come to know that we can give and receive love; we can teach and be taught. We can exchange wisdom and knowledge in a loving, healthy, mutual manner.

Healing becomes viable and salvific for us and for our community. When we blossom, grow, and heal, those around us also receive a blessing. All of us have issues that make our lives like a mobile. Change one element in the mobile and the entire device is affected. This is also true when we begin to heal. When we begin healing in one area, our entire lives are affected. With healing, we can move through life with a refreshed sense of well-being. We then begin our days with thanksgiving and joy, and those moments follow us throughout the day.

In sum, trust is the process of feeling safe and respected with a healthy sense of dependence and certainty in a covenant relationship with God and others. To trust is to have confidence. To heal and grow requires that we learn to love, trust, and respect ourselves. When we learn how to listen to the Spirit within us and trust ourselves, we can begin to trust others.

## Reflecting and Recording

What was your first experience of trusting someone? When did you first learn that you cannot trust everyone? Were you an adult or a child? How was the situation handled? How do you feel about it now?

How would you describe your relationship with God? Was there ever a time when you lost faith in God and felt that you could not trust God again? How did you resolve this challenge?

Who are the wise women in your life? Do you trust them? Does your trusting them connect with you designating them as wise women?

What are two areas in your life that you would like to change? If you place those concerns in a framework of trust, wisdom, and love, could you come to a greater awareness and perhaps begin the healing process?

**Daughter-Friend Moment**

How can you teach trust to a young woman? See what happens when you really listen to her and she is honest with you. Ask her what it means to trust someone. Ask her to contrast someone who is trustworthy with someone who is untrustworthy. Create an analogy or metaphor for your combined definition of *trust;* then, write a two-page short story with the goal of teaching about trust.

# DAY FIVE: VALUE

*Happy are those who find wisdom, / and those who get understanding, /
for her income is better than silver, / and her revenue better than gold. / She is
more precious than jewels, / and nothing you desire can compare with her. /
Long life is in her right hand; / in her left hand are riches and honor. / Her ways
are ways of pleasantness, / and all her paths are peace. / She is a tree of life
to those who lay hold of her; / those who hold her fast are called happy.*

*(Proverbs 3:13-18)*

A few years back, popular musician Bobby McFarin produced the hit single,
"Don't Worry, Be Happy." With his genius and uncanny ability to use his own
voice to create the sounds of other instruments and the whistling that framed
the tune, you could not help but smile, get a bounce in your step, and feel
lighter when hearing the tune; and these feelings were infectious. In one way,
the poet of this proverb tells us the same thing with a twist. Instead of men-
tioning worry, the poet focuses on wisdom. This proverb demonstrates the effi-
cacy of gaining wisdom and understanding. In other words, as we learn more
about God and life, and as we gain bits of understanding about who we are and
why we are here on this phenomenal planet earth, we can move toward happiness. To be happy is to be content, at peace, aware of who we are and what we
are about as we come to accept our priorities and purpose, which affords us the
opportunity to take appropriate actions. To be happy is to experience blessing.
Conventional wisdom notes that happiness is not a particular destination or a
place but a process.

31

Thus, gaining wisdom and understanding and letting these experiences have an impact on our lives regarding what we think and feel and how we act can bring us to serenity. To navigate this entire ongoing, lifetime process, we have to decide that it is important for us to embrace these challenges. Setting priorities enable us to get to this level of participation, which means that we make decisions about who and what we value, and how much that value relates to others. Sometimes we get into trouble when our criteria for making life decisions are faulty or nonexistent. Sometimes we are in so much pain that we depend upon others to tell us what to do, when to do it, and even how to do it. When we try to better order our priorities in a healthy manner, we choose to be overcomers rather than victims. By doing so, we can determine our own personal ethics.

Ethics defines the type of human behavior upon which we place value. In the United States, we contend that all children should have a solid education. This country, by placing a value on solid education, has placed a value on children receiving instruction and being given opportunities for creative engagement. Consequently, we assess property and other taxes to defray the cost of this education. The behavior that generates the income to support schools, organizing community infrastructure to deliver the educational experience, and recruiting the best possible teachers and administrators to do the ministry of education is ethical behavior. We value our children, therefore we place a high premium on educating them. Problematically, we don't practice the belief that all children should receive a good, competent education. If we did, there would not be high school and college students and athletes graduating without being able to read. In addition, we have lost the sense of a holistic, well-rounded education; otherwise we would require high schools to provide four years of physical education and programs in so-called extracurricular activities, (for example, music, the arts, driver's education, and so forth). We would require our children to be well-rounded, educated, and self-sufficient. Therefore, we would be willing to help pay for a well-rounded, education. Some of the wisdom for us related to the concept of "pay now or pay later" has not yet soaked in.

The poet of the Proverbs reminds us that we need to reassess our value systems so that we can be happy. One cannot put a price tag on happiness or blessing. The happiness that comes from wisdom and understanding has more value than silver, gold, and jewels. In addition to basic human needs like food and shelter, most people see relationships as more important than other tangible things people want but do not need to survive and thrive in order to be happy.

Where we place our priorities shows us what has value to us, and we pay a price. Happiness requires commitment and work to come to fruition. All relationships, even sick or codependent relationships, demand work, hard work, consistent work, loving work. At the same time, we must know how to set appropriate boundaries as we work to craft a loving relationship with our own selves. A loving relationship with one's inner self is a prerequisite to having loving relationships with others. Interestingly though, deciding where we place value does not mean that we have to do without to the point of being in dire straits. Sometimes we can have our cake and eat it too. Finally, the experience of truly having happiness and blessing is inseparable from our walk or active, vital relationship with God.

A life yoked with God is a blessed life. In making God our first and foremost priority, as the center of our lives, we can achieve a balanced serenity. Sure, chaos occurs, bad things happen, and pain is everywhere. The good news about God's presence in our lives is that we understand that we are not in control or in charge; God is. As we focus on our relationship with God, by surrendering all to God, not in sacrifice but in expectation and joy, we experience a heightened sense of wisdom, of blessing. With blessing comes peace and opportunities to minister in love, through justice work.

Aileen Clarke Hernandez, business executive, feminist, and public affairs counselor, in her 1971 address to the National Organization of Women (NOW), reminded us of important values as they relate to our humanity. Finding value and building relationships is part and parcel of becoming healthy persons. In this process of becoming, we recognize that, yes, our individual values and concerns are important; but to become a fully, actualized being, we need to make sure that we help to address societal needs also. She reminds us that to engage ourselves at this level means we place *humanity* at the top of our list rather than masculinity. For women to support men does not mean that we need to become subservient, or sacrifice our dreams and goals, or value ourselves less. How can anyone value us, if we do not value ourselves?

Blessing and happiness via wisdom creates an aura of pleasantness and peace. The tree of life, as a metaphor for wisdom, symbolizes a good life, or fulfilled hope. The engagement of such wisdom is a gift from God, which we must honor and safeguard. Experiencing the gifts of peace and embracing wisdom provide an opportunity for us to reach the height of desire: to be one with God. What blessed assurance to know God, to know blessing, to not worry and be happy!

To know value, then, is to be deemed worthwhile or worthy to self and others. When ascribing value, one engages in a process of blessing and renewal. We value that which is important to us; we make it a top priority. One experiences many types of value on a daily basis. Relying on wisdom, one usually can make good decisions, decisions of value and meaning, tempering the damage that could possibly result from unintended consequences.

## Reflecting and Recording

Get comfortable and do a series of deep breaths for a few minutes. Now list 20 synonyms (words or phrases) for happiness or blessing.

For each of the 20 words, list a color that comes to mind. Then, note how that color provides you with new understanding about *wisdom, blessing, trust,* or *happiness.*

If you were going to select your own living "tree of life," what kind of tree would it be and why? What other memories connect with that particular tree that makes it a good image for you?

What is your earliest *and* most recent experience of someone breaking your trust or betraying you? If you had focused on God when being in relationship with that person, could God-given wisdom have warned you that it was a mistake to connect with that person? Or is this a case where you had no control over the events that occurred? Is it now time and are you willing to "let go and let God" begin to heal in this situation?

## Daughter-Friend Moment

Think about two or three activities that you could participate in with your daughter-friend that would bolster her self-esteem, could draw you closer together, and could strengthen the trust that you share with one another.

# DAY SIX: GENEROSITY

*Do not be afraid of sudden panic, / or of the storm that strikes the wicked; / for the LORD will be your confidence / and will keep your foot from being caught. / Do not withhold good from those to whom it is due, / when it is in your power to do it. / Do not say to your neighbor, "Go, and come again, / tomorrow I will give it"—when you have it with you. / Do not plan harm against your neighbor / who lives trustingly beside you. / Do not quarrel with anyone without cause, / when no harm has been done to you. / Do not envy the violent / and do not choose any of their ways; / for the perverse are an abomination to the LORD, / but the upright are in [divine] confidence.*

*(Proverbs 3:25-32)*

We often hear the word *generosity* in the context of church and other relationships, but what does *generosity* mean? *Generosity*, as an act of love, is an attitude of openness and compassion that supports and helps others. We learn the depths and breadth of generosity by reflecting on God as our model. That we are made in God's image *(Imago Dei)* does not mean that we are God, or can become God. We do, however, have the capacity to do wonderful, generous things. God has given us many gifts of creativity, love, joy, support, and intellect. God has given us capacities to taste, touch, see, hear, and smell as well as the capacity to enjoy the vast awesomeness of creation. Because God has given us so much, and because God loves us so, we never need panic. Whenever life overwhelms, disappoints, or stresses us, if we can step back, breathe deeply, and remember that God cares for us—that God will never, ever forsake us—we need never panic or lose hope.

We need never lose hope because of God's spirit of generosity. When we personify that same God-given spirit of generosity, we then have the capacity to be sensitive to the reality of giving without a need, want, or desire to receive anything in return. We are able to give and resolve our debts when services are rendered. We ought not to postpone payment of debts or in-kind services when the moment dictates immediate action. Sometimes when people who also happen to be our friends do things for us, the adage, "a servant is worthy of his or her hire" (Luke 10:5-7) goes out of the window. We wish unilaterally to change a business transaction into a favor. In this case, we are allowing our relationship to cloud our ethical judgment. When we have the resources to give after the work has been done, it is the time to give. At the same time, we ought *not* ask for things to be done unless we can pay for them on completion, or barring the immediate payment, we will already have a payment agreement in place.

Similarly we ought to pray for a person in the moment when they request prayer and not wait until later. To pray for others is an act of loving generosity. Too often people ask us to pray for them, and we say, "Yes, we will," but then we never get around to doing it. We mean well, but our own lives are so full that we just forget. To avoid such oversights, the generous thing to do is to pray for them immediately. Prayer changes things. Just knowing we cared enough to pray in that moment is reassuring to the one in need. Scripture reminds us that God has no human hands but our hands, no human eyes but our eyes, no human words but our tongues, and no human ears but our ears. Thus, when a person is in need of prayer, we stand as witness on behalf of God and of our community as we minister to someone. At the same time, we must appreciate people's boundaries and not overstep them.

When we respect the boundaries of others, of our neighbors, then we are less likely to do harm; in the words of Robert Frost, "Good fences make good neighbors." We are all developing at different rates. We come from different backgrounds. Some of us did not grow up in homes where a spirit of generosity was important. While financial resources may have been limited, others did grow up with that spirit of generosity because there was so much love, compassion, and caring. People spent time talking to one another, listening, and doing chores, playing sports, and going on outings together. When we fail to respect the boundaries of others, we are no longer generous. Boundary breaking sometimes results from neediness, covetousness, or plain insensitivity. Some of us take everything personally. We cannot discriminate between when we need to act and speak and when we need to be silent and prayerful. While good fences may very well make good neighbors, we want to be careful that the boundaries we raise around our hearts do not close us in even more.

When we hit the boundary wall and begin to act out because people have not heard us, or we feel slighted or used, we react. Many times, when our own boundaries are breached, we feel wounded and are uncertain as to how to proceed. Our people skills are lacking when it comes to disappointment, discomfort, or pain. Sometimes all we can think to do is to respond with anger, out of our own pain. But why squabble for the sake of quarreling? What good, what purpose does anger, squabbling, or quarreling serve? In many instances, quarreling simply escalates the tension and fails to benefit either party. This is not an invitation to be a doormat, or to retreat within, or to deny the effects of obnoxious behavior from other persons. Rather, it is an opportunity to ask: What's really going on here? How important is this argument anyway? What do I hope to gain if I win the argument? Is it better to lose one battle but win the war?

In these situations, we have an opportunity to be generous, to determine what our priorities and values are, and then to live by them. In assessing our own needs and what is important to us in our relationships, there are two issues to avoid: *violence* and *envying those who live violent lives.* Violence destroys, decimates, and diminishes capacities, relationships, and life itself. Violence occurs in horrific cases of genocide, war, and multiple vehicular homicides. Violence also occurs when we use our tongues and voices to hurt others. Even if we say that we are sorry or if we apologize, the pain resulting from the violence of the words and how the words were spoken can be long-lasting. Saying we are sorry seeks and demands forgiveness from the other party; it does not make amends or acknowledge a wrong against the other party before asking forgiveness for ourselves. We need to be better stewards not only of our time and financial resources but also of the way we express ourselves through verbal and body language.

One reminder from folk culture that pertains to this situation is an old adage that says "God don't like ugly." In this proverb we encounter irony and playfulness. God, who created us all as *Imago Dei,* has found this creation to be good; and God loves us. Yet, God does not want us to do ugly things to each other. That which is ugly negates, tears down, and defeats. Ugliness emerges in the form of jealousy, envy, hate, and strife. One helpful motto that shifts the power of "doing ugly" is one from the medical field, "Do no harm." What would happen if we began and maintained each day thinking, "In loving generosity for God, life, me, and for others, I will do no harm." Living by this motto offers us an opportunity for making each day a new beginning.

In sum, generosity is a gift of love, an attitude of openness and compassion that undergirds healthy relationships. Generosity embraces the Spirit of God and shores up our capacity to do wonderful, supportive things for ourselves and others. We are able to have the capacity to share respect with others and to live one day at a time. In generosity, we have hope for new beginnings, for transformation, and for healing.

## Reflecting and Recording

Think back to your childhood and ask yourself: Who were the people who best displayed generosity on a daily basis? What are the traits that they had in common? Is there one person who overwhelmingly stands out on that list? If so, why?

Write two proverbs: (1) a proverb of gratitude and thanksgiving and (2) a proverb that focuses on your ability to enhance your capacity to be generous.

Rewrite Proverbs 3:32-35 in language that you could share with (1) a senior citizen and (2) a child. What is important in how you interpret generosity to them?

Reflect on what you find puzzling or challenging about a generous life. What would have to change for you to be more generous? Do you have the opposite problem? That is, are you too generous? If so, what must you do to change?

## Daughter-Friend Moment

Together construct a short story about women being generous to other women. Create a variety of characters, develop your story line with a goal in mind and limit the story to three pages.

## DAY SEVEN: GROUP MEETING

Prepare for today's meeting in quiet, restful activities. Think about what you have learned and what you would like to share. Remember your group members in prayer and prepare yourself to hear what they have to say as well as what God is saying to you.

# Week Two:
# Measures of
# Applied Wisdom

## DAY ONE: GIFT

*The beginning of wisdom is this: Get wisdom, / and whatever else you get, get insight. / Prize her highly, and she will exalt you; / she will honor you if you embrace her. / She will place on your head a fair garland; / she will bestow on you a beautiful crown."... / My child, be attentive to my words; / incline your ear to my sayings. / Do not let them escape from your sight; / keep them within your heart. / For they are life to those who find them, / and healing to all their flesh. / Keep your heart with all vigilance, / for from it flow the springs of life. / Put away from you crooked speech, / and put devious talk far from you. / Let your eyes look directly forward, / and your gaze be straight before you. / Keep straight the path of your feet, / and all your ways will be sure. / Do not swerve to the right or to the left; / turn your foot away from evil.*

*(Proverbs 4:7-9, 20-27)*

In the theatrical and cinematic musical classic *The Sound of Music*, one of the songs opens with the line: "Let's start at the very beginning, a very good place to start." The poet of the Proverbs reminds us that in choreographing our way through the gift and grace of wisdom we, too, must start at the very beginning. The beginning of obtaining wisdom (*Sophia*) from the Holy Spirit is to be in intimate relations with God. Wisdom begins with listening to the traditions in our families, regarding who and what God is and how God operates in the world. Tradition can be a beautiful gift to present to future generations. Tradition can also be cumbersome and deadly if we make it a *god,* or if the traditions no longer have value or are oppressive.

When embracing God, we embrace wisdom. When we are open to God's wisdom, we gain insight, so that we are cognizant of what is important to keep and what we need to reject or discard. When gaining insight we can be blessed, but only if we prize insight and live accordingly. If we embrace insight, then insight will honor us with gifts of wisdom. When we listen for insight from our elders and ruminate over their words to us, we can have a powerful awakening by holding their healthy words of wisdom close to our inner selves. What is essential is the listening, the discerning, and then the holding of the elders' wisdom words and God's wisdom words close to us. These wisdom words of empowerment then become our outermost and innermost garment simultaneously.

During this process, we are to be steadfast as we embrace the treasures of wisdom, of life. Sometimes it is so easy to stick with a plan, to be wise, to go with the adrenaline rush of gusto—whether we're trying to lose weight, save money for a trip, learn how to sew, or develop a second business. When things go well, we are elated and feel good about life. But what do we do on the difficult days, when all of our planning seems to have been in vain? What do we do when despite all of our best efforts we encounter a series of roadblocks that hinder our dream goal? These are the times when we must just show up and go forward one day at a time. These are the moments when we must not give up, for signs of our progress are often just beyond the horizon. Moreover, if we make the most of the process, then we can see our daily triumphs. If for some reason we do not accomplish our original goal, we can see that our effort has not been wasted and all is not lost.

When we feel that our work and effort has been in vain, the poet of the Proverbs invites us to avoid all ugly, devious talk. In her Pulitzer Prize-winning novel, *The Bluest Eye*, Toni Morrison reminds us of the pathological, cancerous results of fixating on perceived ugliness. When we fixate on what is alleged to be ugly, we breed hate, not love. When we develop rituals and mindsets that glamorize internal and external ugliness to the point of self-pity, we die from the inside and self-destruct. Without appropriate love and support, we can even lose our sanity.

On a daily basis, many of us do not realize what a profound gift we have in the ability to think and express sane thoughts; and how truly blessed we are for it. Recognizing our lives and times as a gift, we can move forward and celebrate the opportunities that lie in the moment and ahead of us. No sacred text of any faith tradition ever said life would be easy or fair. Some of the choices that we make or that are made by others for us cause great pain and difficulty, and they leave us to deal with the intended and unintended consequences. While we need not worry about the past, we do need to learn from what has already occurred. George Santayana reminds us: "Those who cannot remember the past are condemned to repeat it." In addition, we should not worry about the future, for the future is God's time.

Focusing on the font of wisdom, on *Sophia*, we can move into holiness and away from evil. Holiness transmits awe and peace. Ultimate intimacy with God, where God is our first resource, is our first port of call when we must navigate rocky seas. Conversely, God is also first when we honor and give thanks on hearing great news. Our magnificent Power of All Powers dwells in the realm of sacred empowerment, the place where we can really be ourselves, where we bask in wisdom. Someone once said that as difficult as it is to really be ourselves, it is even more difficult and costly not to be. When we give ourselves the gift of being with God, and the gift of truly being ourselves, we live with joy, peace, and holiness at the core of our experience.

In sum, gift comes to us in a variety of forms—as the grace of wisdom, as a way to honor life and all creation moment by moment. When we view life as gift, every moment becomes more special. We come to have a deeper appreciation for our capacities to see, think, hear, know, and learn. When our lives and relationships are simultaneously viewed as gift, we come to know life in covenant as rich, grounded, and magnificent.

## Reflecting and Recording

Begin this day by focusing on life as a gift of grace. Keep a running log of every experience that you have that you would qualify as a gift of grace. Pay particular attention to how you feel and how others around you might feel. At the end of the day, write about the lessons you learned.

Think about the gifts you have received during your lifetime. Which gifts have been most rewarding? How do those gifts continue to have a profound impact on you?

We often get caught up in the *"doing-ness"* of life instead of the *"being-ness."* Take an 8-by-11 sheet of paper and cut it into four parts. At the top of each piece, write "COUPON." Allot a particular time value to each coupon (that is, an amount of time that you will spend with the recipient of the coupon). Decide to whom you will give the coupons. Inform your friends or family that they are to redeem them within the month. On your coupon, list the recipients and the amount of time you have agreed to give them. With gratitude, observe your feelings and the reactions of the coupon holders when the coupon is redeemed.

## Daughter-Friend Moment

Think about and then list ways that you can share with your daughter-friend the value of appreciating personal time—loving, pampering, and honoring yourself. Plan an afternoon out together and share this list with her.

## DAY TWO: CHOICE

*Drink water from your own cistern, / flowing water from your own well. / Should your springs be scattered abroad, / streams of water in the streets? / Let them be for yourself alone, / and not for sharing with strangers. / Let your fountain be blessed, / and rejoice in the wife of your youth, / a lovely deer, a graceful doe. / May her breasts satisfy you at all times; / may you be intoxicated always by her love.*

*(Proverbs 5:15-19)*

The imagery of water in our reading is powerful and brings to mind many life experiences. Water symbolizes life, renewal, and oasis; it is the opposite of arid, dry, empty, or thirsty. When we think of water, we imagine waterfalls, lakes, streams, ponds, seas and oceans, wading pools, Olympic water sports, surfing, swimming, diving, boating, and fishing. We use water for bathing, drinking, and cleaning; it is an ingredient in beverages and used in manufacturing and cooking. Water signifies balance, life, renewal, baptism, and transformation. In Proverbs 5:15-19, water tells a story and is a metaphor for a wife, with the cistern being the marriage bed.

Throughout this proverb, the water imagery intensifies and evokes various scenarios. For example, cisterns or marriages can become polluted. At the same time, according to the text, it is better to have a cistern than no water at all. Moreover, because of the arid nature of the environment in Palestine, one would not wash water down the streets, since such an action would be wasteful. In the hot, dry climate of Palestine, water, a scarce commodity, brought joy and life. Wells and cisterns were not easy to come by, so they required effort to access and maintain.

47

Taken together, the above imagery describes one's spouse as a genuine gift, a blessing, as well as a partner for sexual satisfaction and fertility. But what if we don't have, need, or want a spouse? A contemporary reading of the text illustrates that the water imagery symbolizes partnership and commitment, a loving, life-giving companionship with one's self and a significant other. Consider the example of Ruth and Naomi: Ruth pleaded with Naomi to let her remain: "Where you go, I will go; / Where you lodge, I will lodge; / your people shall be my people, / and your God my God" (Ruth 1:16).

After a healthy, intimate relationship with God, our next most valuable relationship needs to be with ourselves. Some of us have already discovered that we are our own best friend, while others have never really appreciated the gift of our own company and thus have lives that are out of balance. We give, give, and give, yet neglect to take time for ourselves. We see ourselves as sacrificing for the good of others, but are so tightly wound to the point of snapping with anger, resentment, and meanness. When we give too much to others and not enough to ourselves, we put our well-being in a precarious, out-of-balance position. Jessie [Jacquetta] Hawkes, English writer and archaeologist, notes in her book *A Land* that we try to live fragile existences balanced skittishly between an awful quagmire and infinite space. Today's proverb calls for *choice*, the choice of self-care.

Choosing self-care requires us to create healthy boundaries for ourselves. This does not mean that we need to become hermits, or that we cannot have friends and do things for others. However, we must not do for others at the expense of ourselves. Women have been and are socialized to be self-giving, to the point that we think nothing of putting ourselves last. Often we learn too late that we, and our loved ones, pay a heavy penalty. We can become whiney, sarcastic, or needy; and often delusional and self-deceptive. Too often we react with anger, hurt, or disrespect rather than responding with grace and kindness. We lose our capacity for a life of *elegance in wisdom*. Elegance in wisdom is not a matter of wealth and class but is instead a matter of health and dignity. Before we can embrace and bond with each other in healthy companionship, we first need to embrace ourselves with love and appreciation. We must learn to love ourselves before we can attempt to love others.

Only when we have learned to love ourselves unconditionally and fully appreciate who we are can we begin to know the experience of gratitude in a totally new and blessed way. We can then come to appreciate the gift of our minds and hearts and bodies. We celebrate the thousands of little things that we have come to take for granted: smelling a rose; tasting honey; pointing our toes; stretching before getting out of bed; having clear thoughts; balancing our checkbook; learning to smile, feel, love, pray; and knowing God. We take so much for granted, while often judging ourselves quite harshly at times. When we begin the lifelong process of knowing and appreciating ourselves, then we have room and space to love others with all of our senses and to love a significant other physically, sensually, and sexually.

We are to know the passion and pleasure of sexual love as part of a life united with a loving God. Such knowledge requires commitment, maturity, compassion, and care. Wisdom teaches that for all good things, there is a time and a place. We begin by learning first to love ourselves and know what makes us feel good, what gives us pleasure; then we can be open to another mature, loving, committed person. Sexual love is sacred love, is holy and of God. It should never be entered into lightly, without thought, care, and a balanced sense of who we are, whose we are, and why we were created.

Thus, balance is an ongoing daily goal for wholeness and serenity. In reflecting on the properties of water, it symbolizes life, renewal, baptism, balance, and transformation. To balance life is to have a clear, healthy perspective about our use of time, resources, and self. When we fail to exercise balance, we put our well-being in jeopardy. When we focus on balance, we exercise our choice, our capacity to choose; part of that choice is in accepting our gift of sexuality. Balance is a place of peace and serenity, freely chosen in love.

## Reflecting and Recording

Spend some time engaging in free association around the concept of healthy sexual love. What is healthy in sexual love for you? Are there experiences in your past that need to be acknowledged and need to heal before you can be open to spiritual, healthy, sexual love?

Open the Song of Songs at random and begin reading any verse of this sacred and erotic love poem, understanding that this book pertains to love between two people sexually. If you can, let your imagination run freely; see where it takes you.

Write a letter to your spouse or a close friend. Use expressive words and imaginative language. Make a date for an evening focused on the five senses, begun with prayer and candlelight.

## Daughter-Friend Moment

In our culture, we tend to be terrified, embarrassed, or titillated by sex. Think of ways that you can help your daughter-friend accept her sexuality as a gift that she can appreciate and be responsible for.

## DAY THREE: DISHONESTY

*There are six things that the LORD hates, / seven that are an abomination to him:*
*/ haughty eyes, a lying tongue, / and hands that shed innocent blood, / a heart*
*that devises wicked plans, / feet that hurry to run to evil, / a lying witness*
*who testifies falsely, / and one who sows discord in a family. . . . /*
*Can fire be carried in the bosom / without burning one's clothes? /*
*Or can one walk on hot coals / without scorching the feet?*

*(Proverbs 6:16-19, 27-28)*

The claim of dishonesty means that someone or something is less than truthful, which breaks one of the canons of the Ten Commandments—that we should not lie. Lying can occur by omission or commission—something someone did or did not do. God is displeased when we choose to lie and be dishonest, or when we use our body (physically or metaphorically) to do wrong. God hates such disingenuous activity to the point that it is an abomination to God, an atrocity and disgrace. What an indictment!

God must be scandalized, troubled, and grief-stricken that we humans are so disobedient and often arrogantly so. The sage of this proverb describes self-aggrandizing eyes, a lying tongue, destructive hands, and feet that run to evil. The list includes acts that result in death to the human spirit, mind, and body, from arrogance to abuse.

Many of us can remember a time when we believed and spread vicious gossip about another, or occasions when we did not take a stand and refuse to be a part of malicious gossip about others. We might remember a time when we

51

heard racial, sexist, or classist slurs and did not take a stand. Such incidents can also occur in our own neighborhoods when we decide we don't want to live next to "those people," whom we have never met and really do not know at all, because we don't want property values to plunge. What happens when the situation reverses and *we* become "those people"? Consider the famous quote of Pastor Martin Niemöller about moral failure in the face of the Holocaust:

> First they came for the Communists, but I was not a Communist, so I said nothing. Then they came for the Social Democrats, but I was not a Social Democrat, so I did nothing. Then they came for the trade unionists, but I was not a trade unionist. And then they came for the Jews, but I was not a Jew, so I did little. Then when they came for me, there was no one left to stand up for me.

Both those we deem *other* and those we deem *us* are God's people. God does not want God's people hurt and wounded or in pain. If we are honest with ourselves, we recognize that we don't want God's people to hurt either. We all have personally experienced the mountaintops of joy and the deep valleys of pain. If we have reasonable intelligence and the capacity to feel, we will quickly come to see that when we inflict pain on others, we are also inflicting pain on ourselves. We are committing slow emotional, spiritual suicide, for we are smothering the holiness, the God-presence within.

One of the many ways of impeding and spoiling the holiness within our selves is to lie through our actions. Some people steal, some kill, others commit adultery. The old folk adage, "If you lie, you will steal; and if you steal, you will kill," is on the mark. The deeper we descend into deception or delusion, the more slippery the slope, and the easier it is to do even worse things to avoid detection. Telling the truth about how one feels may be uncomfortable, but it leaves room for growth, discussion, and development. The moment we choose to lie, we have to be quite savvy to remember which lies we told to what person. Even if we are never caught, at the end of the day *we* still know that we have lied. Some may say they do not have the *taste* for lying or stealing in and of itself, but aren't acts such as committing adultery another form of lying and stealing?

The last two verses of today's reading refer to being faithful in marriage. To commit adultery is to lie, to betray a trust. Before entering into marriage, couples are encouraged to work on communication, to learn as much as they can about each other; to learn about the other's vulnerabilities, emotional, mental, spiritual, and physical health; past histories, weaknesses, and propensities. If one partner decides to withhold particular information, the risk of injuring their significant other increases drastically. We must not injure an unknowing significant other just to relieve our own guilt and shame. Just as walking on hot coals will scorch one's feet, betraying a trust in marriage will leave wounds and scars.

In sum, dishonesty harms the human spirit, mind, and body; and simultaneously harms the community. We know when dishonesty is occurring when we view the particular attitude, behavior, or event in light of morality and good faith. People are dishonest through lying, by word or deed. When lies spiral down into deeper delusion and deception, we move further away from right relationship with God and with our neighbor. In all relationships, particularly in marriage, the steps to maintaining honesty and a healthy communication dynamic is to be faithful and to listen well in love and with empathy.

## Reflecting and Recording

List each of the Ten Commandments, leaving several blank lines between them. Without judgment or self-editing, list some times when you have broken a commandment.

Taking the list from Question 1, what has been the result of breaking a particular commandment? Did your acts involve others or cause harm to a person or to a relationship?

Taking that same list, look to see what still lingers, what you have not yet atoned for, and where you still need to experience healing. If you are ready, prayerfully ponder how you might make amends.

## Daughter-Friend Moment

Select one of the Ten Commandments that you would like to reflect on with your daughter-friend. Think of ways in which people tend to break that particular commandment. Ask your daughter-friend to do the same. Share your lists and then talk about ways both of you might avoid breaking that commandment in the future.

# DAY FOUR: SEDUCTION

*[I]n the twilight, in the evening, / at the time of night and darkness. / Then a woman comes toward him, / decked out like a prostitute, wily of heart. / She is loud and wayward; / her feet do not stay at home; / now in the street, now in the squares, / and at every corner she lies in wait. / She seizes him and kisses him, / and with impudent face she says to him: . . . . / "I have perfumed my bed with myrrh, / aloes, and cinnamon. / Come, let us take our fill of love until morning; / let us delight ourselves with love. / For my husband is not at home; / he has gone on a long journey. / He took a bag of money with him; / he will not come home until full moon." / With much seductive speech she persuades him; / with her smooth talk she compels him. . . . / He is like a bird rushing into a snare, / not knowing that it will cost him his life.*

*(Proverbs 7:9-13, 17-21, 23b)*

In Chapters 1 through 7 of Proverbs, we have been hearing words of instruction from parents. In Chapter 7, the poet of the Proverbs contrasts Lady Wisdom and an adulterous woman. (Too bad the poet didn't focus on an adulterous male!) Culturally, the woman of the Hebrew Bible is regarded as the chattel, the property of the father, brother, or husband; hence adultery instigated by her or her accomplice is a form of theft from the rightful owner of the property involved. At times, Proverbs seems condemning and judgmental of women, as if women live in a vacuum all by themselves and do not interact with men. Reading carefully, however, we see that the poet's focus is not so much on gender, socio-historical location, or the use of power as it is contrasting wisdom and foolishness. This text, then, reflects the issue of wisdom and how both women and men apply wisdom to issues of sexuality and seduction.

Seducers as depicted in today's reading are aggressive, perhaps even boorish or uncouth. These seducers, often psychological predators, need to be on the prowl, to assuage the ego, and reassure themselves that they have not been rejected or despised as unworthy of a sexual relationship. They would never imagine or admit that they are the ones who somehow are lacking. Seducers are not limited to single adults. Sometimes married adults, or others in long-term committed relationships, are not willing to do the work it takes to make the spiritual, physical, emotional, social, and intellectual parts of their relationships work.

Some find this type of sex sufficient because there are no connections, no long-term commitments or responsibilities. However, as Christians we must be prayerful and careful in the area of sexuality. Experiences of sexual battery, abuse, and misconduct color how and if one can engage in healthy, committed sexual relations. Too often those who are most vulnerable find themselves in unhealthy or damaging relationships. Seducers can be cunning and quite persuasive. They know how to tempt and lure. When they engage in sexual activity, they think only of themselves rather than viewing sex as communion, as Eucharist before God. In this case, the sacredness of self disappears, and the one being preyed upon becomes an object. When people pursue their own needs exclusively, they become foolish and dismissive of their own sacredness. Ultimately the goal of sexually aggressive men and women must be to temper their fantasies and desires within and outside of their committed relationships or marriages. Would that all would be gentle, and cautious, and framed by an appreciation of the sacred gift of sexuality within relationships.

In sum, seduction involves a ritual of enticement that engages the realms of communication, sensual and sexual excitement or stimulation. Such activity is appropriate for consenting adults who are in a committed relationship; such activity between an adult and a minor is never appropriate. Sensuality and sexuality are gifts from God. In all relationships, we must observe appropriate boundaries; we might also invite the presence and wisdom of God long before the seduction occurs in order to make sure that the people with whom we decide to be in intimate relationship are most appropriate for us.

## Reflecting and Recording

When you think of sexual relations and sexual relationships, do you include God in the picture? If not, why not? If so, what has been your experience?

On one side of an 8-by-11 sheet of paper, write "Men" at the top. On the other side write "Women." Divide each side into two columns. Title one column "Sexual Stereotypes" and the other "Sexual Attributes." Make entries in both columns on both sides without much contemplation or editing of your words. Afterwards, reflect on your lists. Think about what your lists say about who you are. Share your lists and reflections with a trusted friend, mentor, or sponsor.

## Daughter-Friend Moment

By the time children reach elementary school, they often have already heard a "street version" of the birds and the bees. What can you and your daughter-friend do now to prepare so that you are not embarrassed or intimidated when children ask questions about sexuality? What can you do to prepare so that you answer the question they ask (and not the one you wished was asked)?

## DAY FIVE: VIRTUE

*The [awe] of the LORD is hatred of evil. / Pride and arrogance and the way of evil / and perverted speech I hate. / I have good advice and sound wisdom; / I have insight, I have strength. / By me kings reign, / and rulers decree what is just; / by me rulers rule, / and nobles, all who govern rightly. / I love those who love me, / and those who seek me diligently find me. / Riches and honor are with me, / enduring wealth and prosperity. / My fruit is better than gold, even fine gold, / and my yield than choice silver. / I walk in the way of righteousness, / along the paths of justice, / endowing with wealth those who love me, / and filling their treasuries.*

*(Proverbs 8:13-21)*

Some concepts in life are pretty straightforward. Others are ambiguous or par-adoxical. Proclaiming that respect for God is the antithesis of evil leaves no room for equivocation. When one respects, loves, and holds God in high esteem, through word and deed, one must be opposed to evil. However, some of us give only lip service to loving and honoring God, finding it difficult to live what we affirm. In today's reading, when we come to learn that respect of God is our foundation and context for daily life, we discover the things that are *not* of God and that God dislikes.

In modern parlance, some of what God dislikes falls into the realm of char-acter defect. God does not like sloth, pride, arrogance, distorted speech, or the embracing of evil. Although we need to have dignity, self-respect, and take pleasure in life, when we are so ego-centered that we believe the source of this

58

awareness is only personal, pride rages and becomes idolatrous. Arrogance is also idolatrous, as one has a haughty and misplaced superiority attitude. True greatness understands the adage, "I am because you are." True greatness also grasps the concept that through grace, love, care, and hard work by others and ourselves, we are privy to certain blessings and experiences that others may never experience. Ultimately, when evaluating attitudes and actions, the question to ask is who or what is the source? If the source is other than God, then we are in trouble.

When connected to and governed by God, we can access power and justice in the appropriate sense. Connecting with God gives us the capacity not only to hear but to discern and listen well. We are able to keep things in perspective and work for balance and serenity.

Those who listen to God and then live by what they have heard can rule and live in just ways. They know the need for balance and building community. Their character is virtuous, and their actions emerge directly from their character. A virtuous life is one that is just, that governs rightly, that works for the community—for the good of the one and the many.

In a relationship with God, where one leads a virtuous life, there are many available gifts. All things belong to God. Hence, whatever or whenever we need something, the first place to check in needs to be with God. God can give us direction in attaining what it is that we believe we need. In that encounter, we may gain clarity about the process of acquisition. We may also learn that what we *think* we need, we do *not* need after all.

The gifts of God are for the people of God, and they are profound and enduring. God's treasure is vast and God wants to share it with us. What treasure is God offering us today? What kind of life are we leading that will help us gain God's treasure?

Virtue then pertains to good assets, characteristics, values, and behaviors. The latter particularly refers to the discipline of ethics, where we focus on human behavior set by a particular standard, in this case, an ethical standard. Virtue undergirds the premise that we will do no harm. Through God's grace, we can experience virtue as righteousness, moral excellence, and the opportunity to choose to live in a meritorious, exemplary manner. With God, we not only can live a virtuous life, but we can access power and justice.

## Reflecting and Recording

Look up the following virtues in a dictionary: *prudence, justice, temperance,* and *fortitude.* Which of these are your strongest virtues? your weakest?

Examine your clothes closet. When was the last time you cleaned it out? Select three items that you are willing to discard and set a date to give them away, blessing someone else in the process.

In the 1920s, America instituted a prohibition against alcohol. Do you drink in moderation, or does your behavior lean toward addiction? Can you identify other addictive behaviors? Pray for the strength to make a change, beginning by letting go and letting God.

## Daughter-Friend Moment

Think of three examples or scenarios that would make good modern-day "parables" for teaching your daughter-friend about virtuous character and living. List these together and plan to share them with others.

## DAY SIX: HOSPITALITY

*Wisdom has built her house, / she has hewn her seven pillars. /
She has slaughtered her animals, she has mixed her wine, / She has also set her
table. / She has sent out her servant girls, she calls / from the highest places
in the town, / "You that are simple, turn in here!" / To those without sense
she says, / "Come, eat of my bread / and drink of the wine I have mixed. /
Lay aside immaturity, and live, / and walk in the way of insight."*

*(Proverbs 9:1-6)*

The poet of this proverb seems to be extending an invitation, which signals the
gift of hospitality and sharing. Hospitality as stewardship is an opportunity for us
to embrace wisdom as central to the core of our being. To embrace such wisdom
is to embrace the love, comfort, and care of God.

Elisabeth Marbury, playwright, literary agent, theater manager, and translator,
in *My Crystal Ball: Reminiscences* reminds us that the welcome of hospitality begins
with room in our heart space, for having room in our hearts means there is room
in our homes where we can embrace God, ourselves, and others. To welcome wisdom
is to create an inner sanctum within our communities and our selves to love
and share with others. Even with our foolishness, Lady Wisdom invites us to
embrace order, just as the world has order. The invitation is to live in harmony
with the rest of creation.

Creation is rife with wisdom. We only have to watch the seasons and note
how plants and animals adapt to changes in temperature, barometric pressure,
heat intensity, and type and frequency of atmospheric moisture. The wisdom in

creation involves a tremendous activity of life and death, of change and surprise. Yet, each spring we know that the tree that shed its leaves several months before will once again produce new foliage. Rosebushes that we cut back during late fall will blossom again, producing a sweet aroma that mesmerizes us.

Wisdom is busy; while folly or foolishness, on the other hand, is lazy and inactive. When we are wise, we are busy and active; and at the same time, we celebrate the appreciation of time and serenity, and we take time to rest and heal. When we are foolish, we often think that there will be no consequences, but we are wrong. Framed by hospitality, the poet of the Proverbs reminds us not to misuse gifts such as power, honor, sex, and wealth. We see the wisdom in such awareness, because we know of the broken lives, the embarrassment, the shame and guilt that emerge when these four gifts are abused.

The writer of this proverb wants us to recognize that because we are of God, we are to be wise. To practice wisdom is to accept the hospitality of Wisdom's house, to be leery of and stay away from the house of Folly. Hospitality and all the attributes of wisdom are a gift. We are thus privileged to walk into the home, the abode of Wisdom. We can live there and dwell always, by God's grace.

In sum, the exercise of wisdom emerges from a context of stewardship and creativity. Wisdom radiates from our heart space, where we make room to give and to receive. We create safe spaces in our homes, churches, and in parks where people can be safe and be received with dignity and respect. Just as creation is rife with wisdom, so we have the opportunity to use that wisdom in sharing hospitality with friends, family, and others.

## Review and Reflection

List three times when the memory of a visit into someone's home makes you smile. What made those experiences enjoyable ones for you?

List three times when you were invited to someone's home, and you did something that was foolish. If you could do it over again, how would you act this time? How can you make amends?

If you were going to design an event that would embody God's wisdom as hospitality, what would you do? Whom would you invite? What would you like your guests to take away from the event?

## Daughter-Friend Moment

Think of three people whom you and your daughter-friend either would like to thank for their hospitality or would like to extend hospitality by sending cards of encouragement, hope, and love. Together, purchase, address, and mail the cards. Conclude your adventure by going to a special restaurant together.

## DAY SEVEN: GROUP MEETING

Prepare for today's group meeting in quiet, restful activities. Think about what you have learned and what you would like to share. Remember your group members in prayer and prepare yourself to hear what they have to say as well as what God is saying to you.

# Week Three: Ethical Reflections on Daily Practice

## DAY ONE: DISCERNMENT

*Hatred stirs up strife, / but love covers all offenses. / On the lips of one who has understanding wisdom is found, / but a rod is for the back of one who lacks sense. / The wise lay up knowledge, / but the babbling of a fool brings ruin near. . . . / When words are many, transgression is not lacking, / but the prudent are restrained in speech. / The tongue of the righteous is choice silver; / the mind of the wicked is of little worth. / The lips of the righteous feed many, / but fools die for lack of sense. / The blessing of the LORD makes rich, / and he adds no sorrow with it. / Doing wrong is like sport to a fool, / but wise conduct is pleasure to a person of understanding.*

*(Proverbs 10:12-14, 19-23)*

*Hate* is such a strong word that when we hear someone say it, we cringe inside. The very thought of harboring such a destructive emotion seems repulsive. After all, isn't hate the opposite of love? Doesn't God command that we love God, ourselves, and our neighbors? We expect bigots and terrorists to hate, but something inside of us dies when we hear a child or an elder utter hateful words. Perhaps, rather than being repulsed by the person, we ought to be inquisitive and reflective. Instead we might ask how we can display love in such a way that this person can come to know love and begin to heal from the pain of inflicted hate. We can also realize that their deep pain is not personal or about us, and perhaps the best thing we can do is to pray that they gain insight and healing. Whatever course we choose needs to emerge from our experience of discernment.

Discernment is a process that takes time and clarity. Often we are impatient and want quick and easy answers for complicated, dense issues. Rarely do we sit still long enough to reflect back and remember that the problem that has become a crisis did not begin this moment but "was a long time coming." That is, the situation was an accident just waiting to happen. When we discern, we realize that correctness is not a zero-sum game: *I do not have to prove you wrong in order to establish that my opinion is right.* A period of crisis and disruption is not the time for blame or shame but for quiet, holy listening or discernment.

Hatred is a fuel, a substance that instigates pain and suffering. Hatred stirs up trouble and misunderstanding; but love can remove hate by discerning the pain behind this destructive energy and can decide if the hateful act needs to be forgiven or simply acknowledged. In our haste to be good Christians, we sometimes rush to give lip service to forgiveness before we have even fully acknowledged the harm and pain caused us by someone doing a hateful act. We don't want to cheapen God's grace by a rush to hasty or inappropriate solutions; it is important to work intentionally through our pain and grief, knowing that only after we acknowledge the extent of the damage done to us, or the damage we have done to others, can there be room for change and healing to begin. We can't heal from something when we are not fully aware of the wrong that has occurred. Merely saying, "I'm sorry," just to appease a parent or friend does not afford one the heart space to experience remorse and openness to change.

In the process of naming the pain of hate, it is also important to understand how to love. Here again is the place of wisdom. For example, how is the rod used to offer support for one with no common sense? The rod is not always about spanking or corporal punishment; it can be the hooked stick the shepherd uses to pull sheep in close. When people are in trouble, they need a discerning, careful ear as a sounding board rather than a beating with a stick. Discipline with love is important as we work to teach and live wisdom in community.

The poet of the Proverbs delivers this message about the power of wisdom and the balance of a life well lived: "The blessing of the LORD makes rich." Note here that *wealthy* is but one synonym for the word *rich*. In the context of this proverb, *rich* could also mean "full, opulent, heavy, fertile, intense," or "ironic." Unfortunately, many of us cannot fully understand such a statement, because we are hustling solely to acquire monetary gain.

In order for our children and grandchildren as well as peers and church members to understand the value of God's riches, we must live the example before their eyes. There is joy in understanding. As Bell Hooks writes in her book, *Teaching to Transgress*, we can know joy in the transferring and retrieval of knowledge in a classroom. There is also joy in engaging in Bible study together, in beginning to see some of the failings of long ago.

In sum, discernment as a tool and a process allows us greater insight into ourselves, our spiritual walk, and the world. Discernment as holy listening takes time and requires the space for empathetic communication. We especially need to rely on the gift of discernment during times of crisis and decision-making, both for ourselves and for others when they are in trouble. Discernment is essential as we continue on our spiritual walk with God.

## Reflecting and Recording

Create a list of words to describe your emotional reactions when you relate to someone you feel has the gift of discernment. Also list words that reflect how you feel when you really need someone's help with discernment and they offer bad advice.

In the day's text, we learned that it is important to operate out of love and not hate, to embrace a life of righteousness and not foolishness. List five things, persons, or events that you hate. Reflect on why you hate these particular items and think about how you can reduce the level of control that they have over you.

## Daughter-Friend Moment

Use a concordance to select a Scripture that pertains to discernment, such as Job 34:3-5, to determine what is good; Psalm 139:2-4, to discern one's going out and lying down; and Philippians 1:9-11, the process of discerning what is best. Read the text aloud with your daughter-friend and note the characteristics of discernment.

List them, and then talk about how each of you can exercise your "discernment muscles" on a daily basis. Rewrite the verses in your own words.

# DAY TWO: HONOR

*A false balance is an abomination to the LORD, / but an accurate weight is [the LORD's] delight. / When pride comes, then comes disgrace; / but wisdom is with the humble. / The integrity of the upright guides them, / but the crookedness of the treacherous destroys them. / Riches do not profit in the day of wrath, / but righteousness delivers from death. / The righteousness of the blameless keeps their ways straight, / but the wicked fall by their own wickedness. / The righteousness of the upright saves them, / but the treacherous are taken captive by their schemes. / When the wicked die, their hope perishes, / and the expectation of the godless comes to nothing. / The righteous are delivered from trouble, / and the wicked get into it instead. / With their mouths the godless would destroy their neighbors, / but by knowledge the righteous are delivered.*

*(Proverbs 11:1-9)*

*Honor* is one of those words that tend to be associated more often with men and with legal and military activities. In addition, we think of honor as in *honor roll*, where people, especially students, are acknowledged for accomplishments, achievements, and good grades. In today's proverb, we think of honor as the capacity to hold ourselves and others in high esteem, to relate to others with integrity and compassion. To do this is to honor the *Imago Dei*, the God within another. We cannot honor God if we fail to honor ourselves and our neighbor.

When we fail to honor others and have a sense of balance in our lives where stability and stewardship are primary goals, then we disappoint God. God hurts when we hurt. Thus, when we spend an inordinate amount of time on certain tasks or relationships at the expense of our relationship with God, we breach our honor with God and ourselves. When we dishonor ourselves with a lack of self-esteem, we dishonor God. There is a big difference between self-esteem and being honorable and the arrogance that springs from inordinate pride and being indulgently self-centered. Pride as ego can lead to self-destruction, as in the saying from Proverbs 16:18, "Pride goes before destruction, and a haughty spirit before a fall." The goal is not self-denigration or false modesty but a clear, reasonable assessment of one's gifts and graces in communion with God and one's community.

Living wisely connects us with honor, greatness, humility, salvation, integrity, and righteousness. Righteousness is beautiful and powerful as it helps to transform hopelessness and desolation. Righteousness also serves as a corrective for the wayward through the good acts and living of the blameless—those who live with honor and integrity. Righteousness extols right living, virtue, and good behavior. On the other hand, wickedness signals certain destruction, failed expectation, and death.

Life is complicated. Many times there are no clear-cut answers, only less-than-perfect choices. For every time that we can find a particular response there are other circumstances that will call that particular response into question. Sometimes the righteous experience God's grace when God rescues them from difficulty. At other times, we recall that passage from Matthew: "[Your parent in heaven] makes [the] sun rise on the evil and on the good, and sends rain on the righteous and on the unrighteous" (Matthew 5:45).

To know God is to experience the mystery of mercy and justice. This experience helps us see options of hope as opposed to coercion and limitation. Making righteous living a habit is to live a life of honor, courage, and dignity. This kind of knowledge is salvific—it saves us from many errors and pain. To live a life of honor is to have an experience of balanced serenity. We get to respect boundaries and to let God be God.

When we think of "letting God be God," we hear echoes of Elijah's sermon in 1 Kings 18:21 on Mount Carmel as he went before the people and said, "If the LORD is God, follow [God]; but if Baal is God, then follow [Baal]." We know that none other is God, but God. God, as Architect of the Universe, spoke all of life into being. Speech as proclamation is powerful, renewing, and life giving. In concert with the gifts of God's creativity, we are to embrace honor as we are mindful of that which we speak. Daily we must ask ourselves, "In thought, word, and deed, do we speak life, or do we speak death?"

In speaking of honor, then, we speak of life with integrity, fullness, grace, nobility, and respect. This respect is for ourselves and for God and holds the covenantal relationship between God, ourselves, and others in sacred trust. Honor, a child of wisdom, also connects with humility, salvation, greatness, and righteousness. A life of honor as righteousness holds life as a gift, embraces intimacy with God, and ultimately can provide us with serenity.

## Reflecting and Recording

Name some women in your life since childhood who have embraced the wisdom of God and the gift of honor and note their attributes.

Name ways in which you have been exposed to or experienced wickedness directed at you. Write a short prayer that names the pain and the possibility for your own hope and spiritual transformation.

List your attributes that pertain to honor. Use these words to write a haiku, a Japanese poem of three unrhymed lines of five, seven, and five syllables respectively.

## Daughter-Friend Moment

Invite your daughter-friend to create a list similar to your list of honorees. Spend time creating handwritten notes to these women and mail them. For any women who are deceased, send family members a note expressing thankfulness for the life of that special woman.

# DAY THREE: CORRUPTION

*The thoughts of the righteous are just; / the advice of the wicked is treacherous. / The words of the wicked are a deadly ambush, / but the speech of the upright delivers them. / The wicked are overthrown and are no more, / but the house of the righteous will stand. / One is commended for good sense, / but a perverse mind is despised. / Better to be despised and have a servant, / than to be self-important and lack food. / The righteous know the needs of their animals, / but the mercy of the wicked is cruel. / Those who till their land will have plenty of food, / but those who follow worthless pursuits have no sense. / The wicked covet the proceeds of wickedness, / but the root of the righteous bears fruit. / The evil are ensnared by the transgression of their lips, / but the righteous escape from trouble.*

*(Proverbs 12:5-13)*

Some days we wonder why we have even bothered getting up; things seem to go from bad to worse. We wake up feeling pretty good about life and about ourselves, then someone meets us with a bad attitude, someone who seems bound and determined to take us down with them. Sometimes the more we try to calm down and get things in perspective, the more the other party has a compulsion to ruffle our feathers. If they succeed, then we get the blame.

This experience may seem insignificant, but sometimes it's the little things that can get us into trouble. We may try to pay little attention to these minor episodes, but cumulatively they eat away at our love of self, God, and others. The author of today's proverb, in writing about the righteous and the wicked, had particular thoughts and advice. One can literally chart or map the thought or attitude and the resulting consequences of righteousness and also wickedness, which in turn can serve as a guideline for how we map and plan our lives, one day at a time.

Connecting ourselves with anything related to wickedness leads to deceit, betrayal, and dishonesty. On a daily basis, most of us would not commit an act of violence with a weapon; but words uttered harshly can and do hurt and hurt badly. Hurtful words originate out of the pain of distorted thinking. Conversely, righteousness calls us to remember that God brought about the Creation through speech, and thus righteous persons can speak in a way that delivers healing.

Being righteous can be infectious as we create a legacy for being anchored in God. "Rootedness," an essential trait of righteousness, allows us to seek balance and be sensitive to the needs of all creation. Righteousness as a framework for life is an opportunity to plan, prepare, work, and reap the rewards. With much of the pastoral and agricultural language of Proverbs 12:5-13, we are reminded that God cares for creation and that as an act of praise we, too, need to be sensitive to our environment. Such sensitivity moves us closer to God and to a keen sense of gratitude.

The essence of a faithful life is no mystery; it involves cause and effect. If one plans, prepares, and works, one reaps rewards. On the other hand, waste begets waste. If we pursue meaningless things, we will reap meaningless things. For those who look for a quick fix to any challenge, they too will end up with a less meaningful solution.

Righteousness is fertile and creative. It provides space for hope, discernment, and truth-telling. Corruption tears down, dismantles, and annihilates. The interesting thing about corruption is that it can wear different masks, masks that are titillating, enticing, and magnetic. Corruption produces more corruption, and it destroys.

Corruption is not something to fear however, but something to name, expose, and seek to transform. If the corruption is something that ultimately we cannot change, then we must learn to handle it in a way that does not overwhelm or destroy us. At the very least we can learn, through prayer and discernment, how to address corruption. When corruption has no power over us, we have more room to allow righteousness to bloom from the inside out. Though the righteous experience difficulty, ultimately they escape from trouble, because they are of God and can have peace and contentment in the midst of consternation.

In sum, corruption is distortion of reality, the practices of vice. When corruption enters our lives, we experience "trauma-drama," where chaos reigns supreme. Little molehills become mountains that overwhelm. Corruption often emerges out of deep pain and fuzzy thinking. Sometimes it is premeditated; other times corruption emerges when someone is at a crossroads. The antithesis of corruption is righteousness. Righteousness calls us to remember the stories of our families and friends, to remember and celebrate our own stories, and to remember that God is a God of deliverance and healing.

## Reflecting and Recording

Using index cards, write one word per card that you associate with *righteousness*. Similarly, write one word per card that you associate with *corruption*. Shuffle the cards and pull cards one at a time from the deck. For each word, think about an instance when you experienced that kind of righteousness or corruption in someone else. Note how you feel about the situation now.

Once again pull cards from the deck. This time, think about when you were the perpetrator or giver of that particular experience. If it was corruption, how can you make amends, making sure to change your behavior? If it was about righteousness, what one thing can you do today to share that experience with someone else?

## Daughter-Friend Moment

Create a short story about corruption with your daughter-friend. Write it, then share it with others.

## DAY FOUR: VIOLENCE

*A wise child loves discipline, / but a scoffer does not listen to rebuke. /*
*From the fruit of their words good persons eat good things, / but the desire*
*of the treacherous is for wrongdoing. / Those who guard their mouths preserve*
*their lives; / those who open wide their lips come to ruin. / The appetite of the lazy*
*craves, and gets nothing, / while the appetite of the diligent is richly supplied. /*
*The righteous hate falsehood, / but the wicked act shamefully and disgracefully. /*
*Righteousness guards one whose way is upright, / but sin overthrows the wicked. . . . /*
*Those who spare the rod hate their children, / but those who love them are diligent*
*to discipline them. / The righteous have enough to satisfy their appetite, /*
*but the belly of the wicked is empty.*

*(Proverbs 13:1-6; 24-25)*

When we speak of wisdom, we often think of people who have lived long
lives, such as prominent thinkers and philosophers, public intellectuals, and
often pastors. Seldom do we equate children with wisdom. Yet, the poet of the
Proverbs begins by celebrating the wisdom of children and their desire for wisdom juxtaposed against the scoffer, who ridicules or mocks. Oftentimes, such
scoffers are in pain and take that pain out on others, consciously or uncon-
sciously causing wrongdoing within and outside of themselves. Wrongdoing of
any sort breaks the relationship between God and self and between the self and
others. Such wrongdoing is violence.

We can exact violence on ourselves and others in many ways. We can also
practice doing good in many ways. Good tends to attract good, just as bad tends

to attract bad. However, life is generally much more complicated and ambiguous than neat categories of good and bad. Sometimes we are too close to a situation to be able to sort through what is good, what is bad, and where the lines blur in the gray areas. Discernment is essential for working through life's complexities. Without it, depending upon what is at stake and where our allegiances lie, we may allow ourselves to be placed in uncompromising situations where our actions are not what we would have desired; and the consequences of those actions can be devastating. Actions of good and bad, of righteousness and treachery often emerge from our appetites.

An appetite for violence to one's own self-esteem allows us to be lazy, cause harm to ourselves, or act in shameful and disgraceful ways. We do grave harm with our tongues when we violate the reputation and feelings of others, causing stress and emotional harm. Because words are so powerful, they have to be controlled. If left unchecked, they can cause harm in the community by hurting our neighbors as well as ourselves.

Conversely, disciplined appetites can be a blessing. Without desire we fail to exercise our imaginations. Without using our imagination, we violate the gifts of hope and possibility. An appetite of disciplined joy involves daily planning, commitment, and steady work, which yield tremendous rewards, beginning with the satisfaction of having blessed God by using our talents for good. Likewise, when we monitor what we say and how we say it, we help to build up rather than tear down. As women of faith, hope, and love, we need to be unceasingly prayerful as we think and then speak. Not everything we think or feel needs to be uttered immediately or even at all. Some of it ought never to be spoken. Instead, it can sometimes be helpful to talk with a friend, spiritual director, or counselor.

Another option for releasing hurtful words is writing in the pages of a diary, since writing is a helpful tool for exploring issues of pain, confusion, and distress. It can also be helpful to write but not send a letter, for example about a difficult co-worker or boss, a cantankerous older parent, a petulant immature adult, or a spouse or partner who is being unreasonable. Trying to stifle emotions can exacerbate the problem and result in deep resentment. Our feelings are not right or wrong, but increased awareness of them goes a long way in helping us cope with difficult situations and difficult people. As with a splinter, once the hurtful words are "pulled out," the healing can begin.

Sometimes we use more than words. When dealing with children, all parents get frustrated from time to time, and some resort to spanking. Some parents may say, "If it was good enough for my parents, it's good enough for me." Is it? Do we want to teach our children that love is painful? Usually when we spank children, we are acting more out of our own anger than reacting to something the child did or did not do. In many instances, the sole benefit for administering physical punishment to a child is to express our own anger, fear, or outrage. Similarly when the child is physically punished, the unintended lesson conveyed is that "might is right." When we are angry, it is not the best time to deal with disobedience. At that point, both parent and child need a "time out." There are other options for disciplining in love.

In sum, violence is that which causes harm. Violence occurs in many ways, from the physical and emotional to the financial and psychological. In the church, one primary realm of violence is verbal abuse. Any such violence breaks relationship between God and self and between self and others. When one engages in self-destructive behavior, there is often a history of pain and deep hurt. The resulting low self-esteem often results in deep stress, shame, and compromised health and social well-being. One must process previous pain to move toward healing. When graced to have a child, one must also be prayerful when meting out discipline. We can use our anger creatively; but when we are in denial about our anger, we often engage in destructive behaviors. When our awareness of our own violent behaviors increases and we decide to move closer to God, with proper spiritual and psychological work we can come to accept who we are, through grace, to change our behaviors and to know joy, peace, and contentment.

## Reflecting and Recording

Read Psalm 6:1 ("O LORD, do not rebuke me in your anger, / or discipline me in your wrath"); then look up the word *discipline* in the dictionary. Note the different meanings of this term and apply them to the psalm. How can you incorporate more discipline in your daily life?

List some acts of violence—physical and otherwise—that you have witnessed this week—on a global, national, state, local, and personal level. Name the violence that has had a direct impact on you. Examine your list and decide one action you can take to limit violence in your life.

## Daughter-Friend Moment

Young people are impressionable and need to be taught how to deal with good and bad life experiences. Share examples of acceptable and unacceptable behavior with your daughter-friend. Together make a list of events that happened today and talk about whether they were acceptable or unacceptable. Identify responses that maintain dignity and respect.

# DAY FIVE: ARROGANCE

*It is the wisdom of the clever to understand where they go, / but the folly of fools
misleads. / Fools mock at the guilt offering, / but the upright enjoy God's favor. /
The heart knows its own bitterness, / and no stranger shares its joy. /
The house of the wicked is destroyed, / but the tent of the upright flourishes. . . . /
The simple believe everything, / but the clever consider their steps. / The wise
are cautious and turn away from evil, / but the fool throws off restraint and is
careless. / One who is quick-tempered acts foolishly, / and the schemer is hated. /
The simple are adorned with folly, / but the clever are crowned with knowledge.*

*(Proverbs 14:8-11; 15-18)*

Marilyn Frye, philosopher and writer, in *The Politics of Reality: Essays in
Feminist Theory,* reminds us that arrogance and love are polar opposites.
Arrogance involves conceit, egotism, and pride. True greatness, on the other
hand, is humble and realizes that the source of its importance, merit, and excellence is a loving God. We are stewards of our gifts and thus ought to show gratitude, not arrogance.

Often when people exhibit arrogance, they wear a mask of superiority because
they have an inferiority complex or lack self-worth. Underneath they are afraid.
They may not realize they come across as arrogant or foolish.

Some people are fools; that is, they are easily deceived, tricked, or bamboozled.
Some of us have been blessed with lots of common sense or "mother wit." We
can see the patterns in life and know how to make practical decisions. Other
individuals have unchecked imaginations with huge dreams but not a clue as to
the steps needed to achieve those dreams.

All of us are foolish at times. Fools do not care about their imagination nor about actualizing all that they are, which allows them to throw caution to the wind. Being lackadaisical, fools are often careless, quick-tempered, and immature.

Living a righteous, thoughtful life is elegant and joyous. Sometimes it is simple: Love God, love self, love neighbor. These simple words are, in fact, a lifetime process. It can stretch us, cause pain, and bring joy. Those who appreciate the gift of a righteous life can experience the elegance of simplicity and know peace. They also can appreciate the giver of these gifts and offer the living of their daily lives as praise.

We live life as praise in order to model this life for others, especially our children. We want them to learn from our wise and foolish acts. We need to be diligent as we daily worship, read, learn, and share our wealth of knowledge and experience. The key to sharing well is to know when to speak and when to listen. How arrogant it is to presume that we, as adults, have all the answers, all the time! Erica Jong notes that "advice is what we ask for when we already know the answer but wish we didn't." When we seek God daily, we will know when to be a quiet presence and when to speak.

In reflecting, arrogance indicates conceit, egotism, and pride, an inordinate pride from a self-centered perspective. Arrogance takes our minds off God and instead focuses on self-aggrandizement. To understand our feelings and to ascertain whether we are arrogant or not requires contemplation and soul searching. When we tap into wisdom, we are able to connect with righteousness and can flourish spiritually. In all things we desire balance, and thus some pride is healthy and needed. When our pride gets out of control to the point of our being self-absorbed, or when we think that we are better than others for whatever reason, we have become imbalanced and take on foolish behavior. By seeking God and doing self-inventory daily, we have a better chance of living a balanced life, tempering our arrogance.

## Reflecting and Recording

Think about some of your favorite characters from movies or books. Can you think of a character who comes across as arrogant? What are that person's particular traits?

List ten synonyms for *arrogance* on a sheet of paper. Next to each word draw a face illustrating that trait.

## Daughter-Friend Moment

The teenage and young adult years can be challenging and difficult, so it is important to help young women bolster their self-esteem and morale. First, reflect with your daughter-friend about her feelings. How would she describe herself? Would she describe herself as arrogant? Where is she healthy? Where does she know pain?

Spend time talking with her about poise, posture, and attire as a way to reflect inner well-being. Help her to see her strengths and formulate a plan for dealing with her weaknesses. At the end of your time together, go out for coffee or tea. Then buy her a flower of her choice as a way of honoring your relationship and showing your appreciation for her friendship. When you give her the flower, include a note thanking her for being in your life.

# DAY SIX: COMMUNICATION

*A soft answer turns away wrath, / but a harsh word stirs up anger. / The tongue of the wise dispenses knowledge, / but the mouths of fools pour out folly. / The eyes of the LORD are in every place, / keeping watch on the evil and the good. / A gentle tongue is a tree of life, / but perverseness in it breaks the spirit. / A fool despises a parent's instruction, / but the one who heeds admonition is prudent. / In the house of the righteous there is much treasure, / but trouble befalls the income of the wicked. / The lips of the wise spread knowledge; / not so the minds of fools. / The sacrifice of the wicked is an abomination to the LORD, / but the prayer of the upright is [the LORD'S] delight.*

*(Proverbs 15:1-8)*

Communication is the process of connecting verbally and nonverbally with others, sharing information between people and groups; one originates, the other receives—and the intention to share is understood. We communicate through words of prose and poetry, through song and sign, through pictures and music, through touch and taste. We communicate intentionally and unintentionally. Communication can be empowering or devastating.

Communication is central to both self-expression and community. Some of the most effective communication comes through gentle, kind speech that can temper rage or anger. Such communication requires knowledge of the audience, a sensitivity to timing, care in the use of particular words, and care in how one speaks, paying attention to pitch, volume, and accompanying body language and gestures. A gentle, kind approach can sooth those who are hurting or in pain. Harsh, vindictive speech blocks communication, often resulting in the listener's taking a defensive posture.

Effective communicators learn how to listen without taking things personally and how to answer without escalating an argument. Ineffective communicators are unaware that their intent is not readily apparent nor reflected in their words or actions. Thus the communication can be received as hurtful. Like all things concerning relationships, communication takes work.

Communication is basic to all walks of life; we want others to relate to us, connect with us, and not ignore us. Every relationship requires communication. We communicate what we think and feel about ourselves in various ways: how we speak, dress, move, and play.

Miscommunication occurs on a daily basis, many times a day; and it often catches us unaware. Miscommunication may be a function of bad timing, inappropriate or unclear language, an imagination run amuck, or an event that causes us to misinterpret what we see. Miscommunication may also pertain to cultural understandings. A gesture that is harmless in one culture may be insulting in another. For people growing up in a large family, yelling as a means of communication may be standard operating procedure. For an only child, it may have a very different meaning.

One of the most important venues of communication is prayer. The prophetic books proclaim that God answers prayer (Isaiah 38:5) and that there are times when a prayer cannot get through (Lamentations 3:8; 3:44). Daniel reminds us of the connections among prayer, petition, and fasting (Daniel 9:3). In the Wisdom tradition, we learn that our prayers do not fall on deaf ears. The psalmists teach us that we can use the imperative or command voice when seeking God's favor (Psalms 4:1). Further, they have a certainty that God will hear our prayers (Psalms 66:19) and answer them (Psalms 102:17), because God has not rejected them (Psalms 66:20). In prayer and in conversation, we have expectations, make assumptions, and hope for positive results.

When we are talking about facts that do not directly affect us, it is easy to maintain an easygoing manner that can be firm without being harsh. When communications involve our emotions, however, sometimes we lose perspective and blur boundaries we need to respect. Communication at such times can be approached prayerfully, recognizing that everyone can have her/his opinion, just as we have ours. Even though our opinions may be diametrically opposed, we can agree to disagree in love, with respect. Because we are "works in progress," there will always be ways we can fine-tune our communication, working to do God's will in our relationships with others.

In sum, communication is an essential component of life in community. This process can be creative and empowering, or it can be critical, useless, and devastating. Communication crosses categories of age, race, gender, ability, and class. Loving, compassionate communication is respectful and never dismisses an individual. Communication can occur through verbal and body language. Communication with God is prayer. One can communicate best when one listens attentively in the moment, without anticipating the statement or bringing in personal biases.

## Reflecting and Recording

Write a paragraph describing your emotional "palette." Which emotions do you tap into on a daily basis? What things trigger your emotions? How do you feel when you express yourself in these ways?

List ten emotions you have felt recently. Then stand before a mirror, read each emotion aloud, and make a face that depicts that emotion. What messages did your expressions in the mirror convey to you?

## Daughter-Friend Moment

Much of our communication is nonverbal, not unlike the game of "Bible Charades." Select three or four Bible verses and communicate them to your daughter-friend without using your voice, asking her to guess the verses. Then switch places and repeat the experience.

## DAY SEVEN: GROUP MEETING

Prepare for today's group meeting in quiet, restful activities. Think about what you have learned and what you would like to share. Remember your group members in prayer and prepare yourself to hear what they have to say as well as what God is saying to you.

# Week Four:
# What Triggers Foolishness

## DAY ONE: RELATIONSHIP

*Those who are hot-tempered stir up strife, / but those who are slow to anger calm contention. / The way of the lazy is overgrown with thorns, / but the path of the upright is a level highway. / A wise child makes a glad father, / but the foolish despise their mothers. / Folly is a joy to one who has no sense, / but a person of understanding walks straight ahead. / Without counsel, plans go wrong, / but with many advisers they succeed. / To make an apt answer is a joy to anyone, / and a word in season, how good it is! / For the wise the path of life leads upward, / in order to avoid Sheol below. / The LORD tears down the house of the proud, / but maintains the widow's boundaries. / Evil plans are an abomination to the LORD, / but gracious words are pure. / Those who are greedy for unjust gain make trouble for their households, / but those who hate bribes will live.*

*(Proverbs 15:18-27)*

We learn a lot about people by observing how they communicate with us and with others. Today's proverb focuses on communication, especially in families. Family relationships can be inspiring or deadly. Parents or guardians mold and shape us as infants and children. Mothers and fathers have an opportunity to share love and attention with their children and with each other. Consider the sad situation where the parent is married to the children at the expense of the spouse. Are such parents wonderful mothers and fathers because they are putting the children first? Yet, isn't this the ideal that is preached in many pulpits and advice columns?

Parents are responsible for their children's earliest training, including faith and general education. Families are the arena where we learn about relationships and experience emotions firsthand. We experience these emotions and begin to connect them with positive or negative reinforcement at home through our interactions with family.

The family also helps us identify our strengths and weaknesses. In families where there are hot tempers, often there are ongoing divisions and strife. In families that are slow to anger, we learn to make calm decisions, to wait for God and garner spiritual guidance in times of stress and chaos.

Many elements are critical to the parent-child relationship, including listening to one another and modeling the best possible behavior for children. When the Scripture says that the sins of the parents are visited upon the children, it does not mean a curse or unlucky inheritance is received at birth; rather, it refers to the fact that children pattern their behavior after what they see, hear, and feel. When parents are inconsistent in their actions, children receive mixed messages; and their behavior shows it.

One way to foster healthy relationships is to surround ourselves with others who are wise. Too often in families we refuse to seek advice and counsel from our elders, grandparents, and great-grandparents. What would happen if each church had a visitation ministry to visit elderly members who are homebound? What would happen if every senior in our church and local community connected with a young adult, youth, or child?

Studies have shown that when daycare centers are next to retirement communities, both seniors and children flourish. Seniors feel valued, and children have the opportunity to connect with older persons. When we are bereft of our seniors' wisdom, we become vulnerable.

The traditional African adage, "It takes a village to raise a child," means that many adults are important to the rearing of a child, not only the immediate, biological family. With family, extended family, and friends, it is always important to listen well and seek advice daily from God and trusted friends, not just when crises come.

Some of the crises in our lives cannot be helped. However, some are of our own making. When we worship false gods, we make someone or something more important than our relationship with God. When we do this, things get out of balance; and God is not pleased.

When we are greedy for unjust gain, we make trouble for ourselves and others. If we are good stewards of our resources, we understand that there is no need to resort to envy or greed regarding what others have. Such negative desires distort our relationships and compromise our love and integrity.

In all relationships, we are to build solidarity through love and justice, setting realistic and faithful priorities. We are to work daily on our relationships with our families, with each other, and with God.

In sum, relationships are pivotal to our entire existence. We build family, friendships, and social interactions based upon relationships. Wisdom is important for us regarding relationships because they can be inspiring or deadly. In dealing with families and personal connections, a gentle, loving approach is critical for helping sustain long-term relationships. For healthy growth and survival of our communities, it is important for us to have an intergenerational connection, so that children will better understand themselves as they understand the stories of their ancestors.

## Reflecting and Recording

Draw a tree on a sheet of paper. Determine the ten most significant relationships in your life and identify them as roots and branches.

Think about the events of your life for the last five years. Make a column for each of these years. In another column next to the date, list a few of the major events of each year. After noting the events, write something about the nature of your relationship with God in a third column. Do any patterns emerge between the events and your connection with God?

When people close to you describe you, what are some of the words they use? Make a list of the words. Which are positive and which are negative? What one trait do you most like about yourself and why? What one trait would you like to change? How will you work on it?

**Daughter-Friend Moment**

Spend time together with your daughter-friend, making a list of the character traits you most enjoy in the other person. Where are you both most vulnerable? How can you help each other?

# DAY TWO: EMOTIONS

*Righteous lips are the delight of a king, / and he loves those who speak what is right. / A king's wrath is a messenger of death, / and whoever is wise will appease it. / In the light of a king's face there is life, / and his favor is like the clouds that bring the spring rain. / How much better to get wisdom than gold! / To get understanding is to be chosen rather than silver. / The highway of the upright avoids evil; / those who guard their way preserve their lives. / Pride goes before destruction, / and a haughty spirit before a fall. / It is better to be of a lowly spirit among the poor / than to divide the spoil with the proud. / Those who are attentive to a matter will prosper, / and happy are those who trust in the LORD.*

*(Proverbs 16:13-20)*

God's grandeur is expressed in the physical world—bright stars, majestic mountain ranges, fragile orchids, giant redwoods, petite hummingbirds, gossamer butterflies, and ocean-going whales. In humans, God's grandeur is expressed in our many colors, sizes, and shapes as well as our capacities to think, do, believe, and invent. Part of being human is the vast palette of divinely given emotions and expressions at our disposal.

Emotions are our feelings, the affective or arousing, moving or touching aspects of consciousness. Emotions involve both physical and psychic reactions. These reactions physiologically can involve deeply rooted chemical changes that prepare the body for immediate action. These changes result in emotions we usually view as negative, including anger, distrust, fear, shame, sadness, and a sense of powerlessness. When these emotions are effectively managed, they can

91

become a resource for effectively resolving conflict. However, when they are not effectively managed, they can intensify a conflict, heightening tensions and making the situation more difficult to resolve. Emotions we experience as positive sensations contribute to transformation and change. They include love, joy, curiosity, wonder, excitement, intrinsic motivation, interest, serenity, tranquility, contentment, and relief. The more aware we are of ourselves and our choices, the more opportunity we have to use our emotions appropriately.

The context for our study of emotions is a theme that we read about in the earlier Proverbs, the contrast between wickedness and righteousness. When we do evil, it is an abomination. Doing evil breaks our covenant relationship with God and compromises our integrity. If we are caught, we are often angry, ashamed, and possibly saddened. When we do justice, we feel contentment, pleasure, and joy.

As described in today's proverb, the attributes of the earthly king or judge mirror those of God, the heavenly king. Seeking God's favor or the king's favor is life giving; it brings bounty and the freshness of a spring rain. Wisdom, involving positive emotions, is better than any monetary wealth. To understand and find value in life, to appreciate one's emotions, is a gift. The alternative is regret: If only I had this or that. If only I had more time and more money. If only I didn't have this problem. One of my favorite sayings that squelches the need to go down the road of such regret is: "Uncle or Aunt 'Would have,' 'Could have,' 'Should have,' or 'Used to' died." This saying is an admonition to live in the present. Rather than go down the road of "if only," we have the option of saying, "Thank God for all that I received today." Twelve-step programs have a saying for helping people hold the past and present in tension: "We will not regret the past nor wish to shut the door on it."

To know wisdom, we must listen well and trust God. To trust God completely, unequivocally, absolutely, positively is gradually to free ourselves from negative emotions and to embrace positive emotions. Like the numerous colors on the color wheel, we have the capacity to experience many emotions on various levels, particularly as we seek wisdom, righteousness, and love.

In sum, emotions are our tapestry or palette of feelings, which reflect our psychological responses to the way we experience the world. Emotions express how various life encounters move, arouse, stimulate, or touch an aspect of our consciousness. We often talk about negative emotions such as fear, anger, distrust, sadness, shame, and powerlessness as well as positive emotions such as wonder, love, joy, curiosity, relief, and serenity. Either set of emotions can lead to transformation or, if we go off the deep end with either set, to destruction. Viewed through the lens of wickedness and righteousness, we must aim for emotional sobriety by experiencing and expressing emotions appropriately. Critical to attaining this balance are these questions: Who am I? Whose am I? What call does God have on my life? What are the impediments to my goals? How can I remain open to God and be led to solutions, hope, and transformation?

## Reflecting and Recording

List ten negative emotions. For each emotion, think of a time you have felt that emotion and describe how you felt.

Make a list of ten positive emotions. For each emotion, think of a time you have felt that emotion and describe how you felt.

What have you learned about yourself from doing these exercises?

**Daughter-Friend Moment**

Discuss with your daughter-friend the subject of positive and negative emotions, letting her lead the conversation and supporting her concerns. If she seems to be stuck, use wordplay or free association involving words such as *love* and *anger*, *sadness* and *joy*. (Wordplay or free association is a technique in which a person selects a word. In response, the other person says words that come to mind. For example, in response to *hot*, someone might say words such as *cold*, *temperature*, *warm*, *heat*, *weather*, or *spicy*.)

# DAY THREE: EVIL

*Evil will not depart from the house / of one who returns evil for good. /*
*The beginning of strife is like letting out water; / so stop before the quarrel breaks*
*out. / One who justifies the wicked and one who condemns the righteous / are both*
*alike an abomination to the* LORD. */ Why should fools have a price in hand /*
*to buy wisdom, when they have no mind to learn? / A friend loves at all times, /*
*and kinsfolk are born to share adversity. / It is senseless to give a pledge, /*
*to become surety for a neighbor. / One who loves transgression loves strife; /*
*one who builds a high threshold invites broken bones. / The crooked of mind*
*do not prosper / and the perverse of tongue fall into calamity.*

*(Proverbs 17:13-20)*

Evil exists in the world and has been a catalyst for many literary and cinematic classics, including the Creation story in Genesis, the Greek tragedies,
Shakespeare's dramas, Mary Wollstonecraft Shelley's *Frankenstein, Buffy the
Vampire Slayer*, and John Berendt's *Midnight in the Garden of Good and Evil*.
Paul declared that even when he desired to do good, evil was always present
with him (Romans 7:17-19). Evil is that which causes harm, oppression, and
destruction. Evil destroys mental, spiritual, psychological, physical, and economic health and well-being.

As women of faith, our call is not to return or repay evil for the evil done to
us; rather, we are to repay evil with good, for our own benefit as well as that of
the other party. If we indeed reap what we sow, then we will continue to receive
evil if we give evil when good has been done to us (Luke 19:21).

Sometimes we express disapproval of others because we are intimidated by them or feel inferior. If we can put these people down, if we can place them in an unflattering light, then we think we will feel better. Sometimes we take short-cuts or substitute money for love and gentle discipline. Fools may believe that they can buy wisdom, but they cannot, and in trying they show their lack of desire to learn.

Bona fide love and wisdom are long-lasting. A friend loves us through good times and bad. A person of wisdom often exudes the greatest humility. In wisdom and love, we can learn to support each other amidst difficulty and celebrate with each other in times of triumph.

Who are we? We are children of God, who come with many gifts and graces and often much pain and difficulty. Even with difficulty we must not be afraid, but be in awe of God, respecting God and us. While we are taught not to do evil to others, we must remember also not to do evil to ourselves. Evil destroys, causes bitterness, and is antithetical to the good, righteous, just, and beautiful. Evil acts and thoughts tear down; while just, righteous, and loving thoughts build up.

In sum, evil is anything that causes oppression, harm, or destruction. Sometimes we do evil through our attitudes, our speech, and our deeds. Evil is the antithesis of anything that is life-giving. Doing evil exacts a huge toll on us as individuals and in community; and it can destroy our mental, spiritual, physical, psychological, and economic health and well-being. Some of us engage in evil because of learned behavior. Some of us do evil out of impulse and fear. While life is a paradox, and bad things happen to good people, God never forsakes us. Further, as long as we live and focus on the Fount of wisdom, we can know hope and healing.

## Reflecting and Recording

As women of faith, we seldom do outrageously bad things but instead do "little" bad things. Name ten little evils that you have observed others doing. Then circle the ones that you have also committed.

The word *evil* spelled backwards is *live*. Name five life-giving practices that you can begin to incorporate into your daily life.

## Daughter-Friend Moment

Sometimes girls and women have been so sheltered that they develop passive-aggressive behavior, in which they are sharp, trite, and bitter in their conversation with others. Create several imaginary scenes with your daughter-friend that involve negative conversations; then help her think creatively about healthier ways to respond.

# DAY FOUR: PERCEPTION

*The mouths of fools are their ruin, / and their lips a snare to themselves. / The words of a whisperer are like delicious morsels; / they go down into the inner parts of the body. / One who is slack in work / is close kin to a vandal. / The name of the LORD is a strong tower; / the righteous run into it and are safe. / The wealth of the rich is their strong city; / in their imagination it is like a high wall. / Before destruction one's heart is haughty, / but humility goes before honor. / If one gives answer before hearing, / it is folly and shame. / The human spirit will endure sickness; / but a broken spirit—who can bear? / An intelligent mind acquires knowledge, / and the ear of the wise seeks knowledge. / A gift opens doors; it gives access to the great.*

*(Proverbs 18:7-16)*

Perception pertains to our awareness and discernment about how we experience life; that is, how we see. Sometimes we don't see, because we do not know what to look for; we get confused between our perceptions about what we see and that which actually occurs. Our readings or insights into what we think or feel and what is actually happening may be diametrically opposed. We usually view the fool and the wise person as polar opposites, although there are times when a fool does tap into wisdom and when the wise person does something foolish. When are we foolish? We are foolish when we speak without first thinking, making statements that can hurt others and ourselves by causing conflict and ruining friendships and reputations.

We hurt ourselves and others when we engage in whispered rumors or gossip. When we gossip, we become busy talking machines, yakking all day, making noises, and clanging like empty cymbals. We often think of gossip as innocent, harmless behavior. Gossipers forget that, though their target may not know their character is being besmirched, God knows what is done and said. What would happen if we perceived our lives as the open books they are? That is, if we realized that God always knows and searches our heart, would we be more mindful about engaging in behavior that is pleasing to God?

People who engage in foolish behavior are usually not focused on God or on living a life of wisdom. Fools desire many things, including wanting something for nothing. They have little desire to work, and are often lazy and filled with sloth. Ecclesiastes 10:18 reads, "Through sloth the roof sinks in, / and through indolence the house leaks." Yet in life, there are no free rides. Everything costs, and someone ends up paying. People who are lazy, who do not want to work, are like thieves. They take, take, take for self aggrandizement, with no thought of how others feel or will fare. Because God created us and has gifted us well, we are to use our gifts in building up ourselves and our communities. *Not* to use our gifts not only disrespects God but ultimately destroys the gifts that eventually dissipate from lack of use. What are our options, if we want to embrace the gifts we have and a life steeped in wisdom?

Wisdom is the province of God, the one who is strong like a tower where we can find sanctuary, rest, and renewal, a haven for the righteous. Basking in the power and strength of God gives us the opportunity to see clearly who we are and what our purpose is. In seeing and hearing through grace, we perceive through a lens of honesty and responsibility.

When we make assumptions in life, particularly about our own importance, we may become arrogant. In Psalm 75:4 we read: "I say to the boastful, 'Do not boast,' / and to the wicked, 'Do not lift up your horn.' " When trapped by our arrogance, our perceptions are also distorted. Arrogance allows us to avoid hearing well and listening with discernment to advice and guidance.

There are many ways to see and experience life. In the process, we come to learn that the world is God's to control, and we are here as stewards of particular gifts and graces. One of our tasks is to embrace life with an openness to God's call, which involves a process of perception and discernment. What is your call?

In sum, perception concerns the state of our awareness and discernment, which shapes how we see and listen and observe. Sometimes we look but don't really see. Sometimes we hear but don't really listen. Perception is significant in intimate relationships, particularly when we both look at the same thing but see differently. It can produce more tension and sometimes hurt feelings. When we "see" through the lens of prayerful discernment, we listen for the voices and themes of wisdom as we reflect and make decisions.

## Reflecting and Recording

What call does God have on your life? How has that call changed or become deeper over time?

We perceive through our senses: sight, smell, touch, taste, and hearing. Do the following exercises and note your thoughts and feelings about your perceptions.

1. In moving about today, pay special attention to the appearance of trees, flowers, and signage.
2. Note how different buildings you enter seem to have distinctive kinds of smells.
3. Run your hands over your clothes in your closet with your eyes closed.
4. Take time to thoroughly chew your meals, paying particular attention to textures and flavors.
5. Note the sounds all around you, including sounds of people and of things.

## Daughter-Friend Moment

With your daughter-friend, adapt the second question to your time together and note differences in perception. Write a poem reflecting your experience.

# DAY FIVE: WEALTH

*Better the poor walking in integrity / than one perverse of speech who is a fool. / Desire without knowledge is not good, / and one who moves too hurriedly misses the way. / One's own folly leads to ruin, / yet the heart rages against the LORD. / Wealth brings many friends, / but the poor are left friendless. / A false witness will not go unpunished, / and a liar will not escape. / Many seek the favor of the generous, / and everyone is a friend to a giver of gifts. / If the poor are hated even by their kin, / how much more are they shunned by their friends! / When they call after them, they are not there! . . . / Those who keep the commandment will live; / those who are heedless of their ways will die. / Whoever is kind to the poor lends to the LORD, / and will be repaid in full. / Discipline your children while there is hope; / do not set your heart on their destruction. . . . / What is desirable in a person is loyalty, / and it is better to be poor than a liar. / The [awe] of the LORD is life indeed; / filled with it one rests secure / and suffers no harm. / The lazy person buries a hand in the dish, / and will not even bring it back to the mouth.*

*(Proverbs 19:1-7, 16-18, 22-24)*

When we hear the word *wealth*, we often think about success, class, and money. We may be content because we are financially comfortable; or we may be close to despair and depression because we are living so close to the edge financially. But there are other kinds of wealth. We can know the wealth of time and of friends. We can experience the wealth of peace and longevity. All of us are wealthy when we experience intimacy with God and the accompanying feelings

101

of gratitude, humility, and serenity. Wealth anchored in God's love is beyond description and has a value that cannot be measured.

Today's proverb turns upside-down the concepts of rich and poor, foolish and wise. That is, the prophetic word makes it clear that people who are rich may, in fact, be rich fools.

Each of us wants and needs nurture, nourishment for the mind, body, and spirit. Wealth, as a metaphor for bounteous living, connotes having a plentiful supply of love, concern, and adequate resources to meet basic needs. Moreover, wealth points to our ability to work in community to generate a sense of stewardship and responsibility wherein we create the capacity to help sustain ourselves and our neighbors.

The opposite of this kind of wealth is poverty of spirit and mind. An impoverished spirit and mind can manifest in many ways. We begin losing the capacity to be kind and loyal to ourselves and the commitments we have made to others. We begin losing track of our core values that rob us of the wealth of serenity and stability. An impoverished spirit can lead to hopelessness. Hopelessness can lead to despair and more self-destruction. With self-destruction comes a wounded spirit and distance from God.

When we move away from God, we lose strength, hope, and stability. Without this central relationship, life gets out of balance. Things become skewed. When we come from a place of denial, desolation, and distress, we lose touch with reality and can no longer see the possibilities before us. We are like the monkey who puts its hand in the coconut and then cannot get it out to put the food in its mouth. We relinquish our wealth and the possibility to have a rich relationship with God.

In sum, wealth is a category involving access to resources including money, time, status, and loved ones. Access to wealth requires an investment of time, skills, and stewardship. Wealth also includes our commitment to God and to following rules, where we live with integrity. In the absence of wealth framed by wisdom, there is a poverty of spirit and mind. An impoverished mind and spirit means the loss of the capacity to be loyal and kind, to make commitments to self and community, or to use one's total wealth wisely. To be truly wealthy we must use all of our resources wisely, work not to live beyond our financial means, make sure we are nurturing our spiritual selves, and daily engage in inspiring our mental selves. In all things, we are to seek God and embrace wisdom.

**Reflecting and Recording**

Make two columns on a sheet of paper. Write "Wealth" at the top of one column and "Poverty" at the top of the other. List ten ways in which you are wealthy. List ten ways in which you are poor.

Take the list you made and circle two items in each column. Under the circled items for "Wealth," write a prayer of thanksgiving. Under the circled items for "Poverty," write ways in which you can turn those experiences from poverty to wealth.

**Daughter-Friend Moment**

Discuss with your daughter-friend her understandings of *wealth* and *poverty*. Note where she feels pain and help her discover options for transforming her impoverishment to a sense of well-being or wealth.

# DAY SIX: HEALTH

*Wine is a mocker, strong drink a brawler, / and whoever is led astray by it is not wise. / The dread anger of a king is like the growling of a lion; / anyone who provokes him to anger forfeits life itself. . . . / Who can say, "I have made my heart clean; / I am pure from my sin"? / Diverse weights and diverse measures / are both alike an abomination to the LORD. / Even children make themselves known by their acts, / by whether what they do is pure and right. / The hearing ear and the seeing eye— / the LORD has made them both. / Do not love sleep, or else you will come to poverty; / open your eyes, and you will have plenty of bread. / "Bad, bad," says the buyer, / then goes away and boasts. . . . / Bread gained by deceit is sweet, / but afterward the mouth will be full of gravel. / Plans are established by taking advice; / wage war by following wise guidance.*

*(Proverbs 20:1-2, 9-14, 17-18)*

Not a day goes by that we don't hear statistics about diseases, viruses, heart rates, longevity, aging, and mortality. HIV/AIDS is pandemic in Africa and has intensified in Asia, Europe, and throughout the Americas. Breast cancer strikes family members, colleagues, church members, and friends. Our stress-filled lives cause increased heart disease and heart failure among women. Our children and young adults are more obese than ever before.

Because our bodies are sacred temples, we are to be good stewards and protect our health. A healthy life is a life of blessing. A life of blessing is a life of balance. A balanced life begins on the inside and flows outward. Such a life requires boundaries, values, and serenity rooted in love.

A healthy life is one where there is self-respect and respect for others. Abuse in any form—verbal, psychological, physical, financial—is unacceptable. We need to determine our values, the concepts and ideals that are important to us, and then live by them, informed by the Holy Spirit.

A healthy life means getting adequate rest, eating appropriately, exercising, living within our means, cultivating friends who love and support us, and monitoring our use of time. Socrates and Plato posited that the Golden Mean—moderation in all things; the middle between the two extremes of surfeit and scarcity—should be our guide.

A healthy life also involves nurturing a rich spiritual life, in which we "take time to be holy." Being intentionally intimate with God rejuvenates us and helps us put life in perspective. Meditation, Scripture study, and prayer are key tools for maintaining our daily connection with God. That connection gives us the wisdom and clarity to be good stewards of all our resources.

A healthy life means keeping the sabbath. In the 21st century, we can easily over-schedule ourselves, leaving little time for God. Even for those of us who do keep the sabbath, we often do so out of habit. We go to church because that is what we do on Sunday. We leave early because we have lunch to prepare or sports to watch. We go to Bible study and prayer meetings because it is on our schedule. Too often we try to get a quick spiritual "fix."

A healthy life is one that has room for spontaneity, fresh anointing, and an infusion of God's grace on a daily basis. A healthy life is open to change and allows us the capacity to grow with God's bidding. Such health leads to a marvelous sense of well-being. If we have chronic medical conditions, spiritual health can improve them and lay the groundwork for a life of peace and serenity.

In sum, health is a state of complete well-being in all aspects of our lives. To achieve this state we must monitor how we participate in life spiritually, mentally, emotionally, physically, and financially. In all things, if we act in prudence and love, trusting in God, we can make the best possible decisions to shore up our well-being. A healthy life is one in which there is respect for God, for self, and for others. If we hold our lives in trust as an act of stewardship, then we can live, be, and do from a place of hope, joy, and contentment, where we honor our total selves as sacred.

## Reflecting and Recording

Do a health assessment. Divide a sheet of paper in half vertically. At the top of the left column write "Assets"; and at the top of the right column write

"Liabilities." List your health assets and liabilities, including physical and spiritual health. Try to have an equal number of items in the two columns.

Reviewing your list of liabilities, choose the one that you feel is most critical and reflect on what you can do either to change the condition or to change your attitude about it.

Reviewing your list of assets, choose one and write a prayer of thanksgiving for it.

## Daughter-Friend Moment

Go for a walk with your daughter-friend and talk about the gift of creation, the gift of health, and the blessing that she is in your life. Create a song celebrating your experience with creation.

## DAY SEVEN: GROUP MEETING

Prepare for today's group meeting in quiet, restful activities. Think about what you have learned and what you would like to share. Remember your group members in prayer and prepare yourself to hear what they have to say as well as what God is saying to you.

# Week Five:
# Paradoxes of
# Daily Encounters

### DAY ONE: JUSTICE

*Do not say, "I will repay evil"; / wait for the LORD, and [the LORD] will help you. / Differing weights are an abomination to the LORD, / and false scales are not good. / All our steps are ordered by the LORD; / how then can we understand our own ways? / It is a snare for one to say rashly, "It is holy," / and begin to reflect only after making a vow. / A wise king winnows the wicked, / and drives the wheel over them. / The human spirit is the lamp of the LORD, / searching every inmost part. . . . / To do righteousness and justice / is more acceptable to the LORD than sacrifice. / The getting of treasures by a lying tongue / is a fleeting vapor and a snare of death. / The violence of the wicked will sweep them away, / because they refuse to do what is just. / The way of the guilty is crooked, / but the conduct of the pure is right.*

*(Proverbs 20:22-27; 21:3, 6-8)*

The language of justice reverberates throughout society. The term is used in myriad ways: the halls of justice, Lady Justice, Justice of the Peace, the scales of justice, "Justice is blind," Supreme Court justices, the US criminal justice system. The term has been defined as "fairness, impartiality, or moral rightness."

*Justice* also has theological meanings. Clearly God is the arbiter of this type of justice, and we are not to decide on our own when and how to do justice. The power of divine justice was expressed in the words of Bridget of Sweden— mystic, author, and nun, who noted in *Revelations of St. Bridget on the Life and Passion of Our Lord and the Life of His Blessed Mother,* that charity, not vengeance, is the source of justice.

The charity of God blesses us in many ways, particularly when we open our-selves to God's leading. Yet, even with that powerful guidance we still cannot truly understand God. How can we possibly understand God, when in many instances we do not even understand ourselves?

The call for justice is a call to righteousness, much like a shepherd guiding a flock of sheep. Wickedness, by contrast, manifests in many forms, including the act of lying. Lying is the death of integrity and justice, since it ultimately produces injustice. Injustice is a form of violence. Violence creates more violence, which in turn leads destruction because the wicked will not do what is just.

Justice, then, is our gift, practice, and law. To do justice for our community and ourselves is to express our love of God. We cannot possibly love God whom we have never seen, if we do not love our neighbor. We cannot possibly love God whom we have never seen, if we do not love ourselves. God is the consummate paradigm or model for love and justice.

Justice is a dynamic force that compels us to do no harm and to stand on the side of the oppressed. Some of the definitions of *justice* include "fairness, good, moral rightness." Justice steeped in charity or love helps us begin to experience liberation. To do justice fully means we need first to be aware of our complicity in violence or injustice. For justice to exist, we need to make a commitment to participating in acts of justice as part of our call to discipleship and to live the Christian life.

## Reflecting and Recording

Justice is a significant issue both in Wisdom Literature (Job, Psalms, Proverbs) and the Prophets. Using a concordance, select one book from Wisdom and one from the Prophets and search the passages for the word *justice*, noting the context in which the word is used.

Select one of the Gospels. Check to see how it uses the word *justice* and how it relates to the life and teachings of Jesus.

What is one thing that you can do to illustrate your appreciation of the prophetic call to do justice?

## Daughter-Friend Moment

Share your findings about the use of *justice* in the Bible (see the first and second activities in "Reflecting and Recording") with your daughter-friend. Ask for her perspective and see what you can learn. Share your appreciation of her as your teacher.

# DAY TWO: INTEGRITY

*A good name is to be chosen rather than great riches, / and favor is better than silver or gold. / The rich and the poor have this in common: / the LORD is the maker of them all. / The clever see danger and hide; / but the simple go on, and suffer for it. / The reward for humility and [awe] of the LORD / is riches and honor and life. / Thorns and snares are in the way of the perverse; / the cautious will keep far from them. / Train children in the right way, / and when old, they will not stray. . . . /*
*Folly is bound up in the heart of a [child], / but the rod of discipline drives it far away. / Oppressing the poor in order to enrich oneself, / and giving to the rich, will lead only to loss. . . . / Do not be one of those who give pledges, / who become surety for debts. / If you have nothing with which to pay, / why should your bed be taken from under you?*

*(Proverbs 22:1-6, 15-16, 26-27)*

*Integrity,* a word we associate with leadership in church as well as politics, involves the capacity of people to adhere to moral or artistic values, sometimes set forth in a code of ethics. *Integrity* means that a person or a thing has solid qualities, which are incorruptible, unimpaired, undivided, and complete. The power of integrity is symbolized by the giving of one's word. If our word, our promises, and our vows mean nothing, then we cannot participate fully in community or stand in faith before God.

Our name also is an important expression of our integrity. Biblically a person's name speaks of character; and having character pertains to exercising integrity. Genesis 12:2 says, "I will make of you a great nation, and I will bless you, and make your name great, so that you will be a blessing."

In training ourselves and our children, it is important to share principles about integrity. To be parents with integrity requires us to act from a perspective of wise love. Raising children can be difficult and energy-consuming, especially as children grow older and their lives become more complex. Many times, we fail to listen to our children; and instead we follow a cookie-cutter approach to child rearing. In addition, too often we live by the "do as I say" approach, so from our children's viewpoint our integrity suffers.

Sometimes it is difficult to maintain one's integrity. Once we begin to stoop, it is much easier to stoop again the next time, perpetrating oppressive behavior to achieve selfish needs, goals, and wants. Whenever one person or group abuses another, we betray our commitment to God, to community, and ultimately to ourselves.

In sum, *integrity* means that a person or a thing has solid qualities, which are incorruptible, unimpaired, and complete. Living our lives with integrity is a faithful journey in which we embrace wisdom and righteousness. We choose to live a life of character out of our sense of faithful integrity. When doing so, we allow our light to shine; and that light reflects the light of Christ in our souls. The road of integrity is one that requires work, focus, honesty, and respect for self and others—where we honor our word and our deeds are right, just, and meaningful.

## Reflecting and Recording

Think back to a time when you felt that someone breeched her integrity. What was the incident? What did you think and how did you feel then? How do you feel about that incident today?

Do a quick analysis of your integrity in three areas: finances, communication, and leadership. Do you have integrity in each of these areas as you relate to others? If not, what do you need to change to feel more positive about your own integrity?

## Daughter-Friend Moment

There is a lot of wisdom in the old adage that "one's word is one's bond." Spend time with your daughter-friend reflecting on the importance of keeping one's word and of not making promises that compromise boundaries that we cannot keep or that would be inappropriate to keep.

# DAY THREE: GREED

*When you sit down to eat with a ruler, / observe carefully what is before you, / and put a knife to your throat / if you have a big appetite. / Do not desire the ruler's delicacies, / for they are deceptive food. / Do not wear yourself out to get rich; / be wise enough to desist. / When your eyes light upon it, it is gone; / for suddenly it takes wings to itself, / flying like an eagle toward heaven. / Do not eat the bread of the stingy; / do not desire their delicacies. . . . / Do not speak in the hearing of a fool, / who will only despise the wisdom of your words.*

*(Proverbs 23:1-6, 9)*

Greed is an insatiable, excessive, or strong desire for wealth or gain. Greed also crosses over into the realm of coveting, an act prohibited in the Ten Commandments. Consider Exodus 20:17: "You shall not covet your neighbor's house; you shall not covet your neighbor's wife, or male or female slave, or ox, or donkey, or anything that belongs to your neighbor."

Today's proverb warns us not to desire, crave, or covet the "delicacies," because what appears to be a delicacy may not be. We should also not work ourselves into a tizzy trying to get rich. Why? We need to have our priorities clear and not focus solely on the desire for financial wealth, in and of itself. The call for wisdom invites us to live and make decisions based on knowing when and how to respond and interact with our neighbors and focusing on our stewardship and love for God.

Greed is the opposite of generosity. Some people resort to greed out of a sense of fear and inferiority. They believe that acquiring things by any means necessary will improve their status. They think that people will respect them more because of what they have accrued. When they do not have legitimate ways to obtain more, they may even resort to theft and fraud.

Greed and stinginess aren't always obvious. Sometimes people have an attitude of greed long before they engage in such activity. For our own health and well-being, it is important that we engage in introspection, that we look inside to see who we are, particularly before calling someone else greedy. We can begin by asking ourselves: *Do I have an attitude of greed? Do I crave attention when others are being applauded? Do I go out of my way to have people notice me at the expense of others? Am I ever satisfied?*

When assessing our "greed quotient," it is also important for us to assess our "wisdom quotient." Some people are born with a great deal of mother wit or common sense; others are not. Some of us are naïve; others are careless. Some of us do not know whom to trust; others seem to have an innate instinct for this.

Ironically, our experience with Jesus the Christ may make us targets for those who are greedy for our faith, our serenity, and the genuine love that we have for others and ourselves.

In sum, greed is a strong, excessive, voracious desire for gain or wealth. We can exercise an attitude and practice of greed in many areas, from financial desire to being in charge of various organizations, businesses, or events. As a person of faith, financial security is appropriate, but the desire for wealth alone is unacceptable. Greed is the opposite of generosity. A healthy goal is for balanced giving and receiving, where we are able to handle our expenses, our time, all of our resources with a commitment to God, ourselves, and our families in thanksgiving.

## Reflecting and Recording

List ten examples of personal greed that you have noticed in yourself or others within the last month. Select two of them and decide how they could have been shifted to reflect generosity.

Using today's proverb, how would you help a pair of young people resolve the issue of sharing accolades, when both have supported and worked on a particular project?

Some people are greedy; some are spendthrifts. If you are working on church projects involving money, how can you resolve the tension that will emerge between people who are polar opposites in the use of finances?

## Daughter-Friend Moment

Setting boundaries and priorities are two important ways of avoiding greed. Talk with your daughter-friend about boundaries and priorities. Help her set goals regarding needs, wants, and desires. These goals can help her develop a healthy attitude concerning balance and generosity.

# DAY FOUR: BETRAYAL

*My child, give me your heart, / and let your eyes observe my ways. /
For a prostitute is a deep pit; / an adulteress is a narrow well. / She lies in wait
like a robber / and increases the number of the faithless. / Who has woe?
Who has sorrow? / Who has strife? Who has complaining? / Who has wounds
without cause? / Who has redness of eyes? / Those who linger late over wine, /
those who keep trying mixed wines. . . . / You will be like one who lies down
in the midst of the sea, / like one who lies on the top of a mast. /
"They struck me," you will say, "but I was not hurt; / they beat me,
but I did not feel it. / When shall I awake? / I will seek another drink."*

*(Proverbs 23:26-30, 34-35)*

The language of betrayal in today's text is powerful, stark, and painful. When people betray themselves or someone else, they desert others in time of need. Betrayal involves seduction, shaming, and disclosure, whether intentional or unintentional.

This proverb sees the prostitute and the adulteress as metaphors for destruction—people who rob, are faithless, have sorrow and strife; who complain and have red eyes because of their penchant for alcohol. Unfortunately, the text does not address why these women have allowed themselves to be put in such compromising positions. We do not know if they were molested or forced into prostitution as teens; we don't know about their financial, psychological, or emotional background. Moreover, the text does not talk about the status of male prostitutes, or of men who commit adultery, only women.

118

Healthy, wise parents work to teach their children values and the import of not engaging in betrayal. Parents try to help children avoid difficult situations such as being in relationships that are harmful or that may skew their sense of boundaries. Unfortunately, when children are too deeply skewed or distorted, they may grow into adults who choose to engage in activities that Scripture deems as folly.

Prostitution and adultery are acts of betrayal for those involved in these activities as well as for their loved one. Moreover, the use of alcohol and drugs generally leads to even more acts of betrayal and manipulation. Supportive and loving compassion is essential for people working to deal with their addictions and the underlying reasons for them. Whatever path a person chooses, it is important to remember to take life one day at a time, grounded in a relationship with God.

In sum, betrayal causes great pain and is an act of shaming, seduction, and disclosure; it pertains to the capacity to disappoint, prove undependable, and be unfaithful. Betrayal occurs in relationships in all aspects of our lives. When someone lies about us or exposes a confidence, they betray us. Those who engage in prostitution and adultery betray themselves by using their bodies for economic gain or an illicit affair. We must be careful in whom we place trust. Before investing our time and energies into relationships, it is important to be candid and to set boundaries and expectations. Under no circumstance can we afford to let anyone or anything compromise our values and integrity.

## Reflecting and Recording

Sometimes we hold onto things for a long time. Are you still holding onto an event or situation in which you felt betrayed by God, others, or yourself? List three that come to mind.

Review the three experiences of betrayal. Select one experience and write your thoughts and feelings about it. Then write a prayer asking God to help you accept what happened.

**Daughter-Friend Moment**

Obtain crayons and butcher block paper. Talk to your daughter-friend about experiences of betrayal. As you reflect on those experiences, express your feelings by creating an artistic work on the paper, together or separately. After you finish the picture, share your thoughts and feelings.

## DAY FIVE: EXCELLENCE

*Do not envy the wicked, / nor desire to be with them; / for their minds devise
violence, / and their lips talk of mischief. / By wisdom a house is built, /
and by understanding it is established; / by knowledge the rooms are filled /
with all precious and pleasant riches. / Wise warriors are mightier than strong
ones, / and those who have knowledge than those who have strength; /
for by wise guidance you can wage your war, / and in abundance of counselors
there is victory. / Wisdom is too high for fools; / in the gate they do not open
their mouths. / Whoever plans to do evil / will be called a mischief-maker.*

*(Proverbs 24:1-8)*

With the quest for wisdom comes the opportunity to achieve a mark of excellence. Excellence pertains to that which is superior, having exceptional merit and goodness. Anything deemed excellent is appealing, exemplary, superb, even transcendent. When we call something or someone excellent, we label the event or the behavior as exceptional, first-rate, outstanding.

In our daily lives, we have an opportunity to embrace an experience of excellence in our work, our spiritual disciplines, our creative play, and our emotional lives. Desiring excellence is not about finding new opportunities to feel stress, setting unreasonable goals and deadlines, or beating up on ourselves. Instead, it involves being good stewards of our gifts and graces as we work for balanced serenity. Part of claiming excellence is learning what feeds our souls and what is detrimental to our well-being.

In considering excellence, a house is an excellent metaphor. A house represents the world that God has constructed for our use and honor. Our bodies can also

121

be thought of as houses, sacred temples crafted by God, temples we are to honor and graciously care for. A house can also stand for any project or relationship that we undertake. Something that is worth constructing, worth engaging, worth planning for is also worth our best care. If we create and build in love, the creation will be strong enough to stand amidst the storms of life, for it will rest on a foundation of excellence.

As stewards who have been entrusted with living on this land, with being in relationship, and with making a contribution to society, we need to be anchored in God as manifested in Christ Jesus. Note that Proverbs is part of the Hebrew canon, or Old Testament. As Christians, our model is Jesus, the incarnation of love, peace, and justice—of excellence.

How can we maintain excellence? Although there are no guaranteed strategies, we can aspire always to seek God first before embarking on new projects and new relationships. The beginning excellence, based in wisdom, is an intimate connection with God.

In sum, excellence is a state or quality of high or superior performance, of having values and virtues that transcend the norm. Excellence is part of our goal for a well-rounded life. Excellence is the framework for our lives as we work to be good stewards of all of the resources God has entrusted with us. When we aspire to excellence, we don't need to be envious or jealous. The quest for excellence allows us an opportunity to be the best steward we can of our God-given resources in a respectful, joyful, prayerful manner.

## Reflecting and Recording

Think of two women you consider to exhibit excellence and the reasons why you chose them.

List some of the sayings you have learned and then discern the wisdom behind them.

Our elders are not the only founts of wisdom; we can also learn a lot from children. Think back and write a phrase or two you have heard from a child and ponder the wisdom behind it. If you cannot think of an instance, listen to a group of young people and see what you can learn from them.

Think about your own abilities and the needs of those you know. Then consider and write down one thing that you can do to bless others as a gesture of excellence.

## Daughter-Friend Moment

Ask your daughter-friend to describe her day or week. Help her discern those points and convergences in her life where she experienced and acted out of excellence.

# DAY SIX: ORDER

*One who gives an honest answer / gives a kiss on the lips. / Prepare your work outside, / get everything ready for you in the field; / and after that build your house. / Do not be a witness against your neighbor without cause, / and do not deceive with your lips. / Do not say, "I will do to others as they have done to me; / I will pay them back for what they have done." / I passed by the field of one who was lazy, / by the vineyard of a stupid person; / and see, it was all overgrown with thorns; / the ground was covered with nettles, / and its stone wall was broken down. / Then I saw and considered it; / I looked and received instruction. / A little sleep, a little slumber, / a little folding of the hands to rest, / and poverty will come upon you like a robber, / and want, like an armed warrior.*

*(Proverbs 24:26-34)*

*Order* is a word we use as a noun or verb, or sometimes as an adjective. An order can be an arrangement, a command to be lawful, or a purchase for goods and services. Order also pertains to classification regarding rank or family— "pecking order"—as well as a particular kind of law or code. An order can be a decree or directive, or it can relate to organizing, contracting for, or regulating. In these various instances, order involves an element of self-imposed control.

Conversely, for God to order our steps we must be willing to relinquish control. We must be willing to wait on God. Sometimes we act impulsively and get ourselves into situations that would not have occurred if we had waited for God to lead.

How amazing and liberating it is to realize that we do not understand everything or *need* to understand everything about life and about ourselves. There is such grace and peace when we are aware of this reality and then move toward acceptance.

In ancient Israel, kings would mediate disputes. Locally, elders or priests would arbitrate disagreements. However, in ancient Israel as well as for believers today the ultimate judge and arbiter was and is God.

The words of the text regarding justice encourage us gently yet firmly to be cognizant of life in community. Vengeance, vindictiveness, and petty jealousy are not part of the agenda. We are discouraged from bearing false witness against our neighbors or lying or trying to deceive others. Such behavior is disorderly. God is in control, despite any chaos we may experience.

The fact that God is in control, however, does not grant us license to be lazy. When one is lazy and work goes undone, our lives become overgrown like weeds. Weeds don't need nurturing, special nutrients, pruning, or watering; but, left unchecked, they can overtake a flowerbed or expanse of grass, turning a formerly manicured lawn into an unkempt pit. A similar pattern occurs in our lives. Everything in life requires effort, care, and maintenance. We must work to keep our spiritual houses in good condition, just as we take care that our physical houses are clean and well kept. The structure where we live as well as the body we inhabit needs care and attention.

Ordering our physical bodies means getting proper exercise, food, support, and sleep. We need prayer, planning, and scheduling that allows flexibility and includes time for rest and relaxation. These guide us toward order and disciplined living. When we take good care of ourselves, we can better serve God and others.

In sum, order pertains to regulating, contracting, and organizing systems, people, or places, where we take care of business, discipline, and movement or strategies based on definite commitments and values. When we focus on God as the author and finisher of our faith, we are able to order our day with grace. Divinely inspired order is important as we live in a world rife with ambiguity, change, and chaos. We can rejoice in freedom and possibility because God is in charge and cares for us. In caring for ourselves, it is important to embrace God and order so that we may engage in creative and healthy living.

### Reflecting and Recording

Take a look at your schedule. Analyze it in terms of time for family, work, pleasure, and ministry. Have you allowed time for God in your daily routine? Is every minute of time scheduled? Does your schedule need to be pared down? What needs to change? Create a new schedule incorporating what you have learned.

Walk through your home. Notice where there is order. What statement do those areas make? Notice where disorder exists and select one small task to accomplish today that will bring more order to your home.

## Daughter-Friend Moment

Teens and young adults, like all of us, often feel stress due to not being orderly enough or being too orderly. Plan to spend time "playing" with your daughter-friend. Notice how order or the lack of it affects your time together.

# DAY SEVEN: GROUP MEETING

Prepare for today's group meeting in quiet, restful activities. Think about what you have learned and what you would like to share. Remember your group members in prayer and prepare yourself to hear what they have to say as well as what God is saying to you.

# Week Six:
# Being Alive,
# Real, and Whole

## DAY ONE: DISCRETION

*Do not put yourself forward in the king's presence / or stand in the place
of the great; / for it is better to be told, "Come up here," / than to be put lower
in the presence of a noble. / What your eyes have seen / do not hastily bring
into court; / for what will you do in the end, / when your neighbor puts you
to shame? / Argue your case with your neighbor directly, / and do not disclose
another's secret; / or else someone who hears you will bring shame upon you, /
and your ill repute will have no end. / A word fitly spoken / is like apples of gold
in a setting of silver. / Like a gold ring or an ornament of gold / is a wise rebuke
to a listening ear. / Like the cold of snow in the time of harvest / are faithful
messengers to those who send them; / they refresh the spirit of their masters. . . . /
If you have found honey, eat only enough for you, / or else, having too much,
you will vomit it. / Let your foot be seldom in your neighbor's house, /
otherwise the neighbor will become weary of you and hate you.*

*(Proverbs 25:6-13, 16-17)*

Discretion involves the capacity and power to make decisions freely. With
discretion, one can responsibly choose a specific course of action after considering the significant facts and circumstances. One can make decisions for good
reasons, in good faith, and in freedom. Critical decision-making involves weigh-
ing various factors, including the dynamics, responsibilities, and politics of the
situation along with possible intended and unintended consequences.
Moreover, discretion allows individuals to weigh when to speak and when to be
silent as well as which battles are important to fight and which are not.

Ecclesiastes 3:1-3 tells us: "For everything there is a season, / and a time for every matter under heaven: / a time to be born, and a time to die; / a time to plant, and a time to pluck up what is planted; / a time to kill, and a time to heal; / a time to break down, and a time to build up."

In numerous situations in order to act and react appropriately, it is important to be aware of rules of etiquette and protocol, to know who has authority and what one's role is. Discretion can help us not to "wear out our welcome." After all, it is better to be invited into a circle than to be dismissed from one.

In doing ministry with various constituencies, it is essential to know not only how to listen but also how and when to speak. Words uttered in love and respect are highly valued and can go a long way in settling disagreements. While a person can offer love, hope, and peace through the use of words of inspiration and concern, words can also destroy and provoke tremendous discord.

Aware of its power, some people intentionally use language to distort and manipulate situations that are already volatile, simply for the sake of asserting their own authority. In these types of exchanges, the role of power has tremendous impact.

Discretion involves appropriate behavior. When in relationships, we have to monitor how we connect, so that we are not sending messages that can be misinterpreted. We not only communicate through speech but through body language as well. When we have a clear awareness of ourselves and our surroundings, we can begin to notice the impact we have on others and the impact they have on us.

Even when we notice our impact on others, discretion is the rule of the day. There is a time and a place for everything; there is a time to listen and a time to respond. With loving discretion, we can respect differences and work to communicate in more effective ways. While we work to squeeze more into our everyday lives, we need to make sure that we don't go overboard with too much work or expectations that cannot be fulfilled. Even too much of a good thing can be destructive.

Discretion, then, is a vehicle for life in moderation. When using discretion, we choose in freedom to make decisions, that is, we have both the capacity and the power to make decisions. Discretion is essential for relationships of leadership and of mutuality. Although we may feel the need to speak or do something, discretion may tell us to be still and be prayerful. Through wisdom, discretion helps us act and react in life with balance and respect for ourselves and others.

## Reflecting and Recording

Think of one ministry you are involved with at your church. Think of some ways you can employ discretion in the services that you perform.

In thinking about doing ministry with the elders or seniors of your church, what particular customs and traditions do you see lacking?

Construct guidelines for talking with children about exercising respect and discretion around family concerns (such as money or health issues).

## Daughter-Friend Moment

Following the Ten Commandments, work with your daughter-friend to create a list of rules for discretion. As a means of achieving a balance between rules and enjoyment, connect each rule of discretion with a rule of joy and fun. For example, one rule of discretion might be the following: I will responsibly keep all confidences to myself, unless someone's welfare is threatened. A corresponding fun rule might be: I will make time to play, when I am not responsible for anyone other than myself.

# DAY TWO: BALANCE

*The lazy person is wiser in self-esteem / than seven who can answer discreetly. /
Like somebody who takes a passing dog by the ears / is one who meddles
in the quarrel of another. / Like a maniac who shoots deadly firebrands
and arrows, / so is one who deceives a neighbor / and says, "I am only joking!" /
For lack of wood the fire goes out, / and where there is no whisperer,
quarreling ceases. . . . / An enemy dissembles in speaking / while harboring deceit
within; / when an enemy speaks graciously, do not believe it, / for there are seven
abominations concealed within; / though hatred is covered with guile, /
the enemy's wickedness will be exposed in the assembly. / Whoever digs a pit
will fall into it, / and a stone will come back on the one who starts it rolling. /
A lying tongue hates its victims, / and a flattering mouth works ruin.*

*(Proverbs 26:16-20, 24-28)*

Balance is an important part of maintaining good relationships. Not all
behaviors are appropriate for all our relationships, as there are degrees of
intimacy. And even within relationships the intensity of the expression of certain
feelings has its time and place. In the Wisdom tradition, as stated in Ecclesiastes,
there is a time and a place for everything under the sun. If we expand the limits
of thinking about time and place, then we have certain protective mecha-
nisms regarding how, when, and why we act. Boundaries, then, are significant
to the practice of balance. Imbalance can manifest in numerous ways.
Imbalance is central to ego-centrism, which is the opposite of loving and caring
for ourselves.

To be ego-centered means we have little regard for anyone else. We cater to our own needs at the expense of others. *Balance,* however, means that we love and care for ourselves as an act of stewardship. Moreover, we are able to be in relationships, giving of ourselves and receiving from others, without harm to either party. When harm comes to our relationships, they are out of balance and signal our broken covenant with God. When our behaviors are skewed emotionally, spiritually, mentally, or physically, we compromise our relationships. To play on the emotions of others is cruel and, like a smoldering fire, causes pain.

Fires may burn passionately within our relationships for different times and different reasons. The fires of agape love help us to grow in God's grace, while the fires of romance warm our heart in ways that kindle joy and help us appreciate the gifts of our sensual, sexual selves. (*Agape* is an ancient term that is frequently used to refer to the primitive celebration of Christian fellowship. It is a higher sense of expressing love, a sense of unconditional, self-giving, universal love, reflecting God's love. This higher sense of agape is beautifully expressed by the apostle Paul in 1 Corinthians 13.)

Conversely, the fires of envy, jealousy, grief, and anger, more often than not, cause pain and destruction. Emotion, in and of itself, however, is not good or bad; the important thing is to channel emotion into positive action. Our first task, then, is to determine where we are emotionally, then come to grip with that reality without feeling bad or wrong. Subsequent tasks are to accept our emotions, reflect on their cause, and then take the necessary steps that will allow us to experience healing.

When we move through the process of life toward healing, it is important to focus on the real issues—what we can change and what should be left to God and others. Not everything that has an impact on our lives requires intent focus. As a gauge we can ask ourselves: *How important is this matter? Is the problem so important that I need to deal with it, or can I bring it to someone else's attention? Is this situation one that will still be important to me tomorrow or next week? If I know that I am correct, how important is it to prove to others that I am right?*

In sum, a life of balance is seasonal and grace-filled. Trying to focus on too much at one time leads to a life of chaos; and doing so is draining, debilitating, and depleting. We cannot help but be weary when everything about us is troubling and out of balance. If we work to get ahead by stepping over others, by digging pits that undermine others, they lose but so do we. When we reap ill will on others, we sow it as well. A life of balance is one of respect and care, of compassion and hope. A life of balance is one where we "do unto others as we would have them do unto us." A life of balance is vibrant; we love ourselves, celebrate community, and embrace gratitude for all that which God has, is, and will do in our lives.

## Reflecting and Recording

Draw a balance scale on a sheet of paper. List various personal traits and habits that you consider positive (credits) on one side, and list those that are negative (debits) on the other side. Is your life in or out of balance?

Select a room in your home. Check for balance of color, lighting, furniture, plants, and so on. Is there clutter that disrupts the design of the room? Rearrange areas that need order and balance.

## Daughter-Friend Moment

Spend time with your daughter-friend assessing your calendars. Do you need to add play time, or delete activities where you are overcommitted? Discuss ways to make changes as a loving, balanced way of caring for yourselves.

# DAY THREE: SELF-AWARENESS

*Do not boast about tomorrow, / for you do not know what a day may bring. /
Let another praise you, and not your own mouth— / a stranger, and not
your own lips. / A stone is heavy, and sand is weighty, / but a fool's provocation
is heavier than both. / Wrath is cruel, anger is overwhelming, /
but who is able to stand before jealousy? / Better is open rebuke /
than hidden love. / Well meant are the wounds a friend inflicts, /
but profuse are the kisses of an enemy. / The sated appetite spurns honey, /
but to a ravenous appetite even the bitter is sweet. / Like a bird that strays
from its nest / is one who strays from home. / Perfume and incense make the heart
glad, / but the soul is torn by trouble. / Do not forsake your friend or the friend of
your parent; / do not go to the house of your kindred in the day of your calamity. /
Better is a neighbor who is nearby / than kindred who are far away.*

*(Proverbs 27:1-10)*

Self-awareness helps us to practice humility and appreciation for ourselves
and others. Etiquette in many circles (and in this proverb) dictates that it is better for someone else to praise us than for us to brag about ourselves. Note carefully the difference between *self-awareness* and *ego-centricism*. Knowing one's
gifts and graces and making statements about them is not problematic. When
these statements become boastful, however, then we have gone too far.

Self-awareness helps us to avoid being foolish. We learn wisdom about our
own needs and desires by focusing on self-awareness. Self-awareness informs us
about who we are and the nature of our wants and needs.

135

The more we know about ourselves, the better we can appreciate how magnificently God has made us. To be aware of our internal and external needs is to grow in grace and mercy. To be aware of these needs means that we loose the shackles of quiet pain and suffering and move beyond denial. Moving from denial to acceptance opens up numerous avenues of acknowledgment, healing, and respect for self and others.

We learn not only to be aware of our own feelings but to wear the cloth of empathy as it relates to others. We learn that while for some "blood is thicker than water," the neighbor that is close by is better for us than our kinfolk who are thousands of miles away. Self-awareness involves consciousness raising and a new intimacy regarding our surroundings.

In sum, self-awareness is the process and capacity of having a deep sense of self from the inside out. Self-awareness helps us to know what we think and feel and how we move in the world. Such a sensibility matures in wisdom as we learn more about ourselves in a way that can support our growth as well as the maturity of others. Self-awareness gives us the capacity to know what we need, to know how to ask for help, and to know how to balance needs and desires as we exercise the gifts of wisdom and the capacity to be content amid chaos, ambiguity, and the unknown.

## Reflecting and Recording

List a favorite color, food, smell, fabric texture, season, time of day, and historical figure. Then review the list. What does it tell you about yourself? Do you like the results? If not, what can you do to change?

What is your favorite Scripture and song? Why are they important to you?

## Daughter-Friend Moment

Ask your daughter-friend to describe herself and describe you in writing. You do the same. Compare notes. What are the similarities and dissimilarities between you?

# DAY FOUR: POWER

*One who augments wealth by exorbitant interest / gathers it for another who is
kind to the poor. / When one will not listen to the law, / even one's prayers
are an abomination. / Those who mislead the upright into evil ways / will fall
into pits of their own making, / but the blameless will have a goodly inheritance. /
The rich is wise in self-esteem, / but an intelligent poor person sees through
the pose. / When the righteous triumph, there is great glory, / but when the wicked
prevail, people go into hiding. / No one who conceals transgressions will prosper, /
but one who confesses and forsakes them will obtain mercy.*

*(Proverbs 28:8-13)*

What is power? Power implies the capability to be in charge; to control other
persons, places, or things; to exert force; to have authority; to order submission
or wield substantial influence. When we have power, we can produce, control,
or influence a particular effect. Consider the psychological effects of confessing
that one is powerless. We can have power in several realms as human beings,
such as in physical strength or intellectual prowess.

Power is a source of energy or a way of accessing it. If we think of our capacity
to make a difference as energy, then we can be less rigid and judgmental. To
have power to do anything is a gift. Though we have the power to make decisions, it is helpful if we are mindful of how we exercise this gift of energy to bless
others. When we are in positions of power and steer those under our influence
into bad behavior, then we are failing. We cause our own doom and may later
wonder what happened. Ultimately our own misdeeds catch up with us. Others
may never know, but we will.

One way to honor the gifts of those we supervise, teach, lead, or do ministry with is to share power with them. Some people are afraid to delegate because of fear and a need to control everything. A wise woman once said, "There's always someone who can do something better than you, and there's always something you can do better than others." In this simple statement there is freedom and there is power.

When righteousness prevails, God receives the glory; and we flourish. We can look to God and gain strength. We can then place things in better perspective. When we focus on the Author and Finisher of our faith, when we look to the hills from whence comes our help, we can rejoice and place ourselves in God's hands.

In sum, power is the capacity to produce, control, or be in authority. Power allows us to access energy and to be in relationship with others, either from a point of mutuality or oppression. Because stewardship and thus power is a gift and responsibility, we must be willing to deal with the intended and unintended consequences of our actions. When we embrace our use of power with wisdom, we come to desire righteousness over wickedness.

## Reflecting and Recording

List the organizations to which you belong. Next, list your responsibilities in those organizations. Take a power inventory by noting whether or not you feel affirmed in each of those settings.

Reflect on the list you made. Does your participation in these organizations still have value for you? If yes, how can you make sure your experience in those groups remains positive?

## Daughter-Friend Moment

Select a beautiful blank card, or create one yourself. On the inside of the card, write words of affirmation and empowerment. Share this with your daughter-friend; then together offer a prayer of gratitude for your empowering relationship.

# DAY FIVE: AUTHORITY

*The poor and the oppressor have this in common: / the LORD gives light to the eyes*
*of both. / If a king judges the poor with equity, / his throne will be established*
*forever. / The rod and reproof give wisdom, / but a mother is disgraced*
*by a neglected child. / When the wicked are in authority, transgression increases, /*
*but the righteous will look upon their downfall. / Discipline your children,*
*and they will give you rest; / they will give delight to your heart. / Where there is*
*no prophecy, the people cast off restraint, / but happy are those who keep the law.*
*. . . / A person's pride will bring humiliation, / but one who is lowly in spirit*
*will obtain honor. / To be a partner of a thief is to hate one's own life; / one hears*
*the victim's curse, but discloses nothing. / The fear of others lays a snare, /*
*but one who trusts in the LORD is secure. / Many seek the favor of a ruler, /*
*but it is from the LORD that one gets justice. / The unjust are an abomination*
*to the righteous, / but the upright are an abomination to the wicked.*

*(Proverbs 29:13-18, 23-27)*

Authority is one of those concepts that make some feel pride and others
quake in their boots. Authority connotes power and control. When we have true
authority, we have confidence in our ability to make decisions, to lead, and to
make a difference. But we ought not to abuse the gift of authority, for God is
the giver and arbiter of authority.

People exercise authority in many places in life: at home, at church, at work,
at play. When God is the authority in the home, then the adults in the home
can share the responsibility of guiding the family as partners. When one adult

is subservient to another, this can cause resentment, hurt feelings, and an imbalance of power.

We are also called to share authority at church and at work. In every instance, our goal is to worship God and to live a life of balanced joy and gratitude. When we do have authority, it is important to protect those who are poor: poor in financial, emotional, mental, physical, and spiritual resources. This protection involves our living a life of righteousness and justice, in which God is the ultimate authority.

Thus, when we exercise our authority, we need to embrace the principles of justice, righteousness, love, and discernment. For example, when it comes to child rearing, it is important to think through values and discipline before the occasion arises where one needs to exercise authority. Many times children misbehave because they feel they have been ignored or left out, that they are unloved, and that no one cares. Sometimes these non-demonstrative ones simply feel bad—they are hurting in some way and do not have the vocabulary nor the discernment to express themselves. In our parental frustration and impatience, we may be tempted to strike out or "spank," using force and fear to coerce a child. This is not the time to react, but the time to breathe deeply, to communicate with the child, and then take steps toward discipline that involves care and patience with God being the ultimate authority. Parenting is not easy; and as the church we need to do a better job at offering adults guidance toward a vision of family, extended family, and the impact of communication.

Having a vision is essential to exercising authority. Vision is our capacity to dream, to visualize, to imagine new and different realities. Without vision we wouldn't have the light bulb, electricity, computers, support hose, microscopic surgery, frozen foods, microwave ovens, or cable television. Vision may be prophetic and revelatory; or it may be based on law, wisdom, and thoughtful instruction. To wield authority appropriately, it is important to have a vision—a sense of what it is we want to do, how we want to do it, and how we can respond to God's call.

We are to live out of the gift of authority with a sense of honor. Walking in the Spirit nurtures that honor. Focusing too much on pride will end in our own destruction. When we do dishonorable things, we put ourselves at risk for more trouble. If we truly trust God for all our needs, wants, and desires, we have an assurance beyond words. That assurance can bring tremendous comfort, particularly when our immediate lives do not seem to provide any answers or insight.

Such comfort sustains us as we become willing to listen for God to speak clearly to us.

In sum, we listen for God and temper the misguided use of authority as we learn to embrace authority and be good stewards of our resources. People exercise authority in many areas of their lives, and each occasion pertains to relationships and well-being. We can live with gusto, give and receive, laugh and cry, rejoice and give thanks.

## Reflecting and Recording

In ordination services, the presider tells the candidates to take the authority to read the Scriptures, celebrate the sacraments, and preach the word. In your own life, where has God given you authority? How have you used that authority?

Think about your own family, social life, and personal life. Where have you noticed a compassionate, responsible use of authority? Where have you seen abuse of authority?

## Daughter-Friend Moment

With your daughter-friend, play a game of charades. Think of words that relate to authority. Using only gestures and movements, see if you can communicate those words to each other.

# DAY SIX: SATISFACTION

*Give strong drink to one who is perishing, / and wine to those in bitter distress; / let them drink and forget their poverty, / and remember their misery no more. / Speak out for those who cannot speak, / for the rights of all the destitute. / Speak out, judge righteously, / defend the rights of the poor and needy. / A capable wife who can find? / She is far more precious than jewels. . . . / Her children rise up and call her happy; / her husband too, and he praises her: / "Many women have done excellently, / but you surpass them all." / Charm is deceitful, and beauty is vain, / but a woman who fears the LORD is to be praised. / Give her a share in the fruit of her hands, / and let her works praise her in the city gates.*

*(Proverbs: 31:6-10, 28-31)*

A classic sales pitch from retailers is "satisfaction guaranteed!" However, so many things in life are not guaranteed, and moments of satisfaction are fleeting at best. Satisfaction is best achieved through a plan for living one day at a time, where God is in control and we are willing to take simple steps toward healthier living. Such balance is important not for our personal satisfaction but for our communal well-being. No one person overcomes obstacles or achieves great things without help from others. Moreover, there is great satisfaction in helping someone else, not for self-aggrandizement but simply for the sake of helping.

Proverbs 31 discusses what makes a wise woman and a wise wife. This wisdom is different from much of Proverbs, which is geared largely to young men who are about to marry. The sentiments of the book are that, just as wise people trust in God, a wise man trusts his wife. Regrettably, some people will use this chapter to limit women to subservient roles.

Who is the woman of Proverbs 31:28-31? The proverb calls her blessed. Her children and husband praise her. Some readings of this proverb place her on a pedestal. However, this position comes with high expectations. Women are no longer allowed to be human, but become objects. Sometimes this feminine ideal has become so transcendent that the average woman could not possibly embody it, nor should she try.

Who should this woman try to satisfy? Others? Herself? God? The great love commandment says to love God first, then to love your neighbor as yourself. After God, we need to learn to love ourselves first. Then we can love our neighbor, whether that neighbor is a spouse, partner, child, sibling, parent, or friend.

In sum, satisfaction involves a sense of pleasure, contentment, joy, or well-being. Satisfaction is also a sense of fulfillment that comes when we can love ourselves well. For true satisfaction, not based on things but grounded in one's state of mind, every woman must be free to be her own best self, give thanks for that best self, and not allow family, society, or her own desires to distort who she is. In all things, she is to love and praise herself, looking to God in gratitude for the strength to love others and appreciate her gift of life. Such a life is truly a life of satisfaction.

## Reflecting and Recording

Take an inventory of your relationships. Are they satisfying for you? If so, why? If not, why? What can you do to enhance your relationships?

List some of the values you think are important for a woman, a wife/partner, and a mother in the 21st century. Note why having these values are important. Can they also be liberating? How do they bring satisfaction?

**Daughter-Friend Moment**

Reflect with your daughter-friend on what it means to experience satisfaction, how women can find satisfaction in the various roles they play in life, and how some roles can be restrictive. Talk about the choices both of you can make, in the context of being a woman of God.

## DAY SEVEN: GROUP MEETING

Prepare for today's final group meeting in quiet, restful activities. Think about what you have learned from this Sisters study and what you would like to share. Remember your group members in prayer and prepare yourself to hear what they have to say as well as what God is saying to you.